Contents

BASIC GO-TO EASY PIZZA DOUGH 4

ELEVATED PIZZA DOUGH 5

SPELT PIZZA DOUGH 6

WHOLE-WHEAT PIZZA DOUGH 8

GLUTEN-FREE PIZZA DOUGH 9

NORTH AFRICAN FLATBREAD 10

ROSEMARY FOCACCIA 11

SWEET DOUGH FOR HAND PIES 13

ESSENTIAL GARLIC OIL 14

SIMPLE TOMATO SAUCE 14

OVEN-ROASTED RED SAUCE 15

CHARRED SWEET PEPPER AND TOMATO SAUCE 15

BASIC PESTO 16

SALSA BIANCA 17

SALSA VERDE 17

WILD FENNEL SAUCE 18

TAPENADE 19

AIOLI 19

HARISSA 20

ANCHOIADE 21

FIG AND ANCHOVY PASTE 21

NUMBER ONE PEPPERONI AND CHEESE PIZZA 21

PIZZA WITH PROSCIUTTO CRUDO, RICOTTA, AND AGED BALSAMICO 22

PIZZA WITH PROSCIUTTO COTTO AND GORGONZOLA 23

PANCETTA PIZZA WITH SWISS CHARD AND ONIONS 24

PIZZA WITH FENNEL SAUSAGE, PEPPERS, AND CALABRIAN CHILES 25

FOUR SEASONS PIZZA 26

SALAMI PIZZA WITH PARSLEY-PARMESAN SALAD 27

FENNEL SAUSAGE AND WILTED GREENS PIZZA WITH FRESH MOZZARELLA 28

WHOLE-WHEAT PIZZA WITH PANCETTA, POTATO, AND ASPARAGUS 29

APPLEWOOD SMOKED BACON AND SUNNY-SIDE UP EGGS WITH PARMESAN 30

PIZZA WITH CHORIZO Y PAPAS, FRESH CILANTRO, AND LIME 31

PIZZA WITH LAMB SAUSAGE, CARAMELIZED ONIONS, AND MARJORAM 32

ALSATIAN-STYLE TART OF STEWED ONIONS, BACON LARDONS, AND BLACK PEPPER 33

FENNEL PIZZA WITH BRESAOLA AND LEMON	34
MERGUEZ FLATBREAD WITH ZUCCHINI, SMOKY EGGPLANT, AND CILANTRO	35
PIZZA WITH CHICKEN SAUSAGE, RED ONIONS, AND CHARRED SWEET PEPPER AND TOMATO SAUCE	35
PIZZA WITH SAN MARZANO TOMATOES AND BRAISED CHICKEN LEGS	36
SHREDDED DUCK LEG AND WINTER SQUASH PIZZA WITH SCAMORZA	38
PIZZA WITH FRESH FIGS, CARAMELIZED ONIONS, AND ANCHOIADE	40
ONION, ANCHOVY, AND NIÇOISE OLIVE PIZZA	41
WHIPPED SALT COD AND POTATO PIZZA	42
FLATBREAD OF SMOKED SALMON AND CAVIAR	44
ROASTED CLAM AND BACON PIZZA	45
SQUID PIZZA WITH CHERRY TOMATOES AND AIOLI	46
SHRIMP, SWEET PEPPER, AND CHERRY TOMATO PIZZA WITH GREEN GARLIC	46
PIZZA MARGHERITA	47
GLUTEN-FREE PESTO PIZZA	48
PIZZA WITH FRESH TOMATOES, GYPSY PEPPERS, AND CAPERS	49
ASPARAGUS AND FAVA BEAN PIZZA WITH TAPENADE	50
EGGPLANT PIZZA WITH FRESH MOZZARELLA AND OVEN-DRIED HERBS	51
WHOLE-WHEAT PIZZA WITH GREENS, RAPINI, PINE NUTS, AND RICOTTA SALATA	52
SQUASH AND SQUASH BLOSSOM PIZZA WITH CHERRY TOMATOES	53
ARTICHOKES, LEEKS, AND GREMOLATA PIZZA	54
ARTICHOKE PIZZA WITH ROASTED RED ONIONS AND FRESH THYME	55
ROASTED BUTTERNUT SQUASH, ROQUEFORT, AND WALNUT PIZZA	56
A GREEN PIE ZUCCHINI, RAPINI, AND PESTO	57
FRESH PORCINI MUSHROOM PIZZA	58
MOREL MUSHROOM PIZZA WITH CREAM AND A SUNNY-SIDE UP EGG	59
STINGING NETTLE AND CHANTERELLE MUSHROOM PIZZA	60
BLACK TRUFFLE AND FONTINA PIZZA	61
THREE-CHEESE CALZONE	62
THREE-MEAT CALZONE	63
THREE-VEGETABLE CALZONE	64
SPINACH, FETA, TAPENADE, AND OREGANO	65
STUFFED AND ROLLED PIZZA RING	66
WINE GRAPE FOCACCIA	67
SWEET HAND PIE OF PUMPKIN, WARM SPICES, AND MASCARPONE	68
SWEET HAND PIE OF ROASTED STONE FRUITS AND FRANGIPANE	69

SWEET HAND PIE OF ROASTED CHERRIES WITH GRAPPA AND AMARETTI 70

SWEET HAND PIE OF BLISTERED APRICOTS, RICOTTA, AND BITTERSWEET CHOCOLATE 71

WARM MONTRACHET WRAPPED IN GRAPE LEAVES WITH ROASTED WINE GRAPES AND FLATBREAD ... 73

OVERNIGHT OVEN-DRIED TOMATOES SOTT'OLIO 74

GRATIN OF WILD MUSHROOM CRÈPES 74

EGGPLANT ROASTED IN THE COALS 76

ROASTED WINTER VEGETABLES IN DUCK FAT AND ROSEMARY 77

LONG-COOKED "POT O' BEANS" WITH OKRA, TOMATOES, AND PEPPERS 77

BAKED EGGS WITH TOMATOES AND DUKKA 78

SHRIMP COOKED IN THE WOOD OVEN WITH GARLIC AND OIL 79

CRACKED LOBSTERS ROASTED WITH PAPRIKA BUTTER 80

WHOLE ROASTED BRANZINO WITH TOMATOES, POTATOES, AND WHITE WINE 81

CANNELLONI WITH SPINACH, LEEKS, AND CHICKEN 82

VIETNAMESE-STYLE PORK SKEWERS IN LETTUCE CUPS 83

RIB-EYE STEAK GRILLED "IN THE WINDOW" WITH SALSA VERDE 84

OVEN-ROASTED FRUITS 85

SIMPLE ARUGULA AND HERB SALAD   SPRING 87

FARM STAND VEGETABLE SALAD   SUMMER 88

LACINATO KALE SALAD WITH CREAMY GARLIC DRESSING AND RADISHES   WINTER 89

BASIC GO-TO EASY PIZZA DOUGH

MAKES EIGHT TO TEN 10-INCH PIZZAS
Prep time: 2 hours, plus up to 24 hours to rise

Ingredients

FOR THE SPONGE
- 1 cup plus 2 tablespoons lukewarm water
- 1 tablespoon active dry yeast
- 4½ ounces (1 cup) all-purpose flour

FOR THE DOUGH
- 1¾ pounds (6½ cups) all-purpose flour
- 2 tablespoons kosher salt
- 1½ cups cold water
- ½ cup extra-virgin olive oil

DIRECTIONS

TO MAKE THE SPONGE

1. Put the warm water in the work bowl of a stand mixer and sprinkle the yeast evenly over the surface. Briefly stir to moisten all the yeast. Add the flour and whisk until no lumps are visible and the entire mixture is moistened. Set the bowl in a warm location.

2. After 30 to 40 minutes, you should notice small bubbles beginning to form on the surface of the sponge and a pleasant "bready-yeasty" smell beginning to arise. If after 40 minutes the sponge does not seem active, wait another 15 minutes and check again. If it still does not seem bubbly and aromatic, discard the sponge and start over, making sure that the water you use is warm to the touch but not scalding and that your yeast is not expired.

TO MAKE THE DOUGH

1. In a large bowl, combine the flour and salt and mix well. Transfer 1½ cups of the flour-salt mixture to the bubbly sponge and add the cold water. Whisk thoroughly and let sit for another 30 minutes.

2. Attach the dough hook to your mixer. Add the remaining flour mixture and the olive oil to the work bowl and knead on medium-low speed for 3 to 5 minutes. Stop the mixer once midway through and push the forming dough off the hook to ensure even kneading. The dough should begin to clean the sides of the bowl, becoming slightly sticky and elastic.

3. Gather up the moist, soft dough ball and transfer it to a large bowl to be left to proof. (If the dough seems too dry, knead it a few times by hand with a few drops of water. If it seems too wet and difficult to handle, sprinkle it with some flour and knead gently to make a manageable dough ball that maintains a slight shape.)

4. Leave the dough in the bowl, cover with plastic wrap or a kitchen towel, and leave in a warm place for about 2 hours. The dough should nearly double in size and become noticeably aromatic. If time allows, the dough will benefit from a long, steady rise in the refrigerator—overnight is best, or even up to 2 days. The flavor will be more complex and the dough will become more pliant with this protracted fermentation process.

5. Either proceed now or, on the following day, punch down the dough by kneading it a few turns on a lightly floured work surface, then divide it into 8 to 10 equal portions, roughly 8 ounces each. Form the dough balls into small pillows by making a circular motion with both cupped hands on a lightly floured work surface. Press and gently turn each pillow to create a seamless round dough ball. (At this point the dough can be wrapped in plastic and frozen for up to a month, then allowed to thaw slowly in the refrigerator before proceeding with the following step.)

6. Arrange the dough balls on a floured tray about 3 inches apart and cover loosely with plastic wrap. Set aside at room temperature to proof for an additional 1 hour. Notice the transformation from dense, cool dough to airy pillows and an increase in the overall size as the dough puffs. You are now ready to shape the dough for pizzas.

ELEVATED PIZZA DOUGH

MAKES EIGHT TO TEN 10-INCH PIZZAS

Prep time: 2 hours, plus up to 24 hours to rise

Ingredients

FOR THE SPONGE
- 1 cup plus 2 tablespoons lukewarm water
- 1 tablespoon active dry yeast
- 4½ ounces (1 cup) rye flour

FOR THE DOUGH
- 13½ ounces (3 cups) 00 flour
- 12 ounces (2¾ cups) all-purpose flour
- 2 tablespoons kosher salt
- 1½ cups cold water
- ½ cup extra-virgin olive oil

DIRECTIONS

TO MAKE THE SPONGE

1. Put the warm water in the work bowl of a stand mixer and sprinkle the yeast evenly over the surface. Briefly stir to moisten all the yeast. Add the rye flour and whisk until no lumps are visible and the entire mixture is moistened. Set the bowl in a warm location.

2. After 30 to 40 minutes, you should notice small bubbles beginning to form on the surface of

the sponge and a pleasant "bready-yeasty" smell beginning to arise. If after 40 minutes the sponge does not seem active, wait another 15 minutes and check again. If it still does not seem bubbly and aromatic, discard the sponge and start over, making sure that the water you use is warm to the touch but not scalding and that your yeast is not expired.

TO MAKE THE DOUGH

1. In a large bowl, combine the two wheat flours and salt and mix well. Transfer 1½ cups of the flour-salt mixture to the bubbly sponge and add the cold water. Whisk thoroughly and let sit for another 30 minutes.

2. Attach the dough hook to your mixer. Add the remaining flour mixture and the olive oil to the work bowl and knead on medium-low speed for 3 to 5 minutes. Stop the mixer once midway through and push the forming dough off the hook to ensure even kneading. The dough should begin to clean the sides of the bowl, becoming slightly sticky and elastic.

3. Gather up the moist, soft dough ball and transfer it to a large bowl to be left to proof. (If the dough seems too dry, knead it a few times by hand with a few drops of water. If it seems too wet and difficult to handle, sprinkle it with some flour and knead gently to make a manageable dough ball that maintains a slight shape.)

4. Leave the dough in the bowl, cover with plastic wrap or a kitchen towel, and leave in a warm place for about 2 hours. The dough should nearly double in size and become noticeably aromatic. If time allows, the dough will benefit from a long, steady rise in the refrigerator—overnight is best, or even up to 2 days. The flavor will be more complex and the dough will become more pliant with this protracted fermentation process.

5. Either proceed now or, on the following day, punch down the dough by kneading it a few turns on a lightly floured work surface, then divide it into 8 to 10 equal portions, roughly 8 ounces each. Form the dough balls into small pillows by making a circular motion with both cupped hands on a lightly floured work surface. Press and gently turn each pillow to create a seamless round dough ball. (At this point the dough can be wrapped in plastic and frozen for up to a month, then allowed to thaw slowly in the refrigerator before proceeding with the following step.)

6. Arrange the dough balls on a floured tray about 3 inches apart and cover loosely with plastic wrap. Set aside at room temperature to proof for an additional 1 hour. Notice the transformation from dense, cool dough to airy pillows and an increase in the overall size as the dough puffs. You are now ready to shape the dough for pizzas.

SPELT PIZZA DOUGH

MAKES TWO 10-INCH OR THREE 8-INCH PIZZAS
Prep time: 2 hours, plus up to 24 hours to rise

Ingredients

FOR THE SPONGE
- ¼ cup plus 2 tablespoons lukewarm water

- 1 teaspoon active dry yeast
- 2 ounces (¼ cup plus 3 tablespoons) spelt flour

FOR THE DOUGH
- 4½ ounces (1 cup) all-purpose flour
- 2 ounces (¼ cup plus 3 tablespoons) semolina flour
- 1 tablespoon kosher salt
- ½ cup cold water
- 2 tablespoons extra-virgin olive oil

DIRECTIONS

TO MAKE THE SPONGE

1. Put the warm water in the work bowl of a stand mixer and sprinkle the yeast evenly over the surface. Briefly stir to moisten all the yeast. Add the spelt flour and whisk until no lumps are visible and the entire mixture is moistened. Set the bowl in a warm location.

2. After 30 to 40 minutes, you should notice small bubbles beginning to form on the surface of the sponge and a pleasant "bready-yeasty" smell beginning to arise. If after 40 minutes the sponge does not seem active, wait another 15 minutes and check again. If it still does not seem bubbly and aromatic, discard the sponge and start over, making sure that the water you use is warm to the touch but not scalding and that your yeast is not expired.

TO MAKE THE DOUGH

1. In a large bowl, combine the all-purpose flour, semolina flour, and salt and mix well. Transfer ½ cup of the flour-salt mixture to the bubbly sponge and add the cold water. Whisk thoroughly and let sit for another 30 minutes.

2. Attach the dough hook to your mixer. Add the remaining flour mixture and the olive oil to the work bowl and knead on medium-low speed for 3 to 5 minutes. Stop the mixer once midway through and push the forming dough off the hook to ensure even kneading. The dough should begin to clean the sides of the bowl, becoming slightly sticky and elastic.

3. Gather up the moist, soft dough ball and transfer it to a large bowl to be left to proof. (If the dough seems too dry, knead it a few times by hand with a few drops of water. If it seems too wet and difficult to handle, sprinkle it with some flour and knead gently to make a manageable dough ball that maintains a slight shape.)

4. Leave the dough in the bowl, cover with plastic wrap or a kitchen towel, and leave in a warm place for about 2 hours. The dough should nearly double in size and become noticeably aromatic. If time allows, the dough will benefit from a long, steady rise in the refrigerator—overnight is best, or even up to 2 days. The flavor will be more complex and the dough will become more pliant with this protracted fermentation process.

5. Either proceed now or, on the following day, punch down the dough by kneading it a few turns on a lightly floured work surface, then divide it into 2 or 3 equal portions. Form the dough balls into small pillows by making a circular motion with both cupped hands on a lightly floured work surface. Press and gently turn each pillow to create a seamless round dough ball. (At this point the dough can be wrapped in plastic and frozen for up to a month, then allowed to thaw slowly in

the refrigerator before proceeding with the following step.)

6. Arrange the dough balls on a floured tray about 3 inches apart and cover loosely with plastic wrap. Set aside at room temperature to proof for an additional 1 hour. Notice the transformation from dense, cool dough to airy pillows and an increase in the overall size as the dough puffs. You are now ready to shape the dough for pizzas.

WHOLE-WHEAT PIZZA DOUGH

MAKES THREE 8-INCH PIZZAS
Prep time: 2 hours, plus up to 24 hours to rise

Ingredients

FOR THE SPONGE
- ¼ cup plus 2 tablespoons lukewarm water
- 1 teaspoon active dry yeast
- 2 ounces (¼ cup plus 3 tablespoons) 00 flour

FOR THE DOUGH
- 9 ounces (2 cups) all-purpose flour
- 2¾ ounces (½ cup plus 2 tablespoons) whole-wheat flour
- 1 tablespoon plus 1 teaspoon kosher salt
- ½ cup cold water
- 2 tablespoons extra-virgin olive oil

DIRECTIONS

TO MAKE THE SPONGE
1. Put the warm water in the work bowl of a stand mixer and sprinkle the yeast evenly over the surface. Briefly stir to moisten all the yeast. Add the 00 flour and whisk until no lumps are visible and the entire mixture is moistened. Set the bowl in a warm location.
2. After 30 to 40 minutes, you should notice small bubbles beginning to form on the surface of the sponge and a pleasant "bready-yeasty" smell beginning to arise. If after 40 minutes the sponge does not seem active, wait another 15 minutes and check again. If it still does not seem bubbly and aromatic, discard the sponge and start over, making sure that the water you use is warm to the touch but not scalding and that your yeast is not expired.

TO MAKE THE DOUGH
1. In a large bowl, combine the all-purpose and whole-wheat flours and salt and mix well. Transfer ½ cup of the flour-salt mixture to the bubbly sponge and add the cold water. Whisk thoroughly and let sit for another 30 minutes.
2. Attach the dough hook to your mixer. Add the remaining flour mixture and the olive oil to the work bowl and knead on medium-low speed for 3 to 5 minutes. Stop the mixer once midway

through and push the forming dough off the hook to ensure even kneading. The dough should begin to clean the sides of the bowl, becoming slightly sticky and elastic.

3. Gather up the moist, soft dough ball and transfer it to a large bowl to be left to proof. (If the dough seems too dry, knead it a few times by hand with a few drops of water. If it seems too wet and difficult to handle, sprinkle it with some flour and knead gently to make a manageable dough ball that maintains a slight shape.)

4. Leave the dough in the bowl, cover with plastic wrap or a kitchen towel, and leave in a warm place for about 2 hours. The dough should nearly double in size and become noticeably aromatic. If time allows, the dough will benefit from a long, steady rise in the refrigerator—overnight is best, or even up to 2 days. The flavor will be more complex and the dough will become more pliant with this protracted fermentation process.

5. Either proceed now or, on the following day, punch down the dough by kneading it a few turns on a lightly floured work surface, then divide it into 3 equal portions, roughly 6 ounces each. Form the dough balls into small pillows by making a circular motion with both cupped hands on a lightly floured work surface. Press and gently turn each pillow to create a seamless round dough ball. (At this point the dough can be wrapped in plastic and frozen for up to a month, then allowed to thaw slowly in the refrigerator before proceeding with the following step.)

6. Arrange the dough balls on a floured tray about 3 inches apart and cover loosely with plastic wrap. Set aside at room temperature to proof for an additional 1 hour. Notice the transformation from dense, cool dough to airy pillows and an increase in the overall size as the dough puffs. You are now ready to shape the dough for pizzas.

GLUTEN-FREE PIZZA DOUGH

MAKES TWO 9-BY-13-INCH PIZZAS
Prep time: 2 hours, plus up to 24 hours to rise
Cook time: 10 to 20 minutes

Ingredients

FOR THE SPONGE
- 1 cup lukewarm water
- ¼ cup whole milk, at room temperature
- 1 tablespoon plus 2 teaspoons active dry yeast
- 1 extra-large egg

FOR THE DOUGH
- 1½ pounds (5¼ cups) gluten-free flour
- 2 teaspoons baking powder, sifted
- 2 teaspoons kosher salt
- 2 teaspoons sugar
- 2 tablespoons extra-virgin olive oil, divided

DIRECTIONS

TO MAKE THE SPONGE

1. In a small bowl, combine the warm water and milk. Sprinkle the yeast evenly over the surface and stir to combine. Set aside in a warm spot until active and bubbly, about 15 minutes.
2. When the yeast mixture is active and bubbly, lightly whisk in the egg.

TO MAKE THE DOUGH

1. Attach the paddle to your stand mixer. In the work bowl, combine the flour, baking powder, salt, and sugar and mix on low speed.
2. Add the bubbly sponge to the work bowl and mix on low speed until combined, 2 to 3 minutes.
3. Gather the dough and transfer to an unfloured work surface. Briefly knead the dough to combine, 4 or 5 turns total.
4. Divide the dough into two equal portions and wrap each tightly in plastic wrap. Gently shape each into a 2-inch-thick disc. Allow to rise in a warm spot for 45 minutes.
5. Preheat the wood oven to approximately 500°F. Brush a quarter sheet pan with 1 tablespoon of the olive oil.
6. Using a wooden rolling pin, roll out the dough on a clean, dry, unfloured surface to ¼-inch thickness, and transfer to the prepared sheet pan. With a sharp paring knife, trim away any excess dough that hangs over the sides of the tray. Fill in any gaps by using the trimmed pieces, pressing the seams together. The entire tray should be filled to the edges. With the tines of a fork, prick the entire surface of the dough.
7. Brush the remaining 1 tablespoon of olive oil over the top of the dough. Transfer to a warm spot and allow the dough to proof for 15 minutes before baking.
8. Bake the dough in a relatively cool zone of the oven, away from the fire, until lightly browned, 8 to 10 minutes, making sure to rotate frequently. Remove the tray from the oven and allow to cool slightly. Add the toppings of your choice and return to the hot oven and bake until warmed through, about 5 minutes more.

NORTH AFRICAN FLATBREAD

MAKES TWO FLATBREADS
Prep time: 2½ hours
Cook time: 2 to 3 minutes per flatbread

Ingredients

FOR THE SPONGE

- ⅔ cup lukewarm water
- ½ teaspoon active dry yeast
- 1 tablespoon extra-virgin olive oil, plus more for topping

FOR THE DOUGH

- 6 ounces (1¼ cups plus 2 tablespoons) 100% whole-grain flour
- 1½ ounces (¼ cup) semolina flour
- ½ teaspoon kosher salt
- 3 tablespoons za'atar (optional; see A Closer Look)

DIRECTIONS

TO MAKE THE SPONGE

1. Put the warm water in the work bowl of a stand mixer and sprinkle the yeast evenly over the surface. Stir to dissolve. Add the olive oil and mix by hand. Set the work bowl in a warm location.
2. After 20 to 30 minutes, you should notice small bubbles beginning to form on the surface of the sponge and a pleasant "bready-yeasty" smell beginning to arise.

TO MAKE THE DOUGH

1. In a large bowl, combine the whole-grain and semolina flours and the salt. Add the flour mixture to the bubbly sponge all at once.
2. Attach the dough hook to your mixer. Mix on medium-low speed until a soft, slightly sticky dough forms and pulls away from the side of the bowl. Continue mixing for 3 minutes. If the dough appears too wet, add another tablespoon of whole-grain flour. If it appears too dry and has a "shaggy" appearance, add 1 teaspoon water. Mix until no lumps appear and you have a smooth dough, about another minute.
3. Transfer the dough to a medium bowl, cover with plastic wrap, and allow to rise in a warm place until roughly doubled in size, 1 to 2 hours.
4. When the dough has risen, uncover and punch it down. Turn it out onto a lightly floured work surface and knead two or three times. Divide the dough into two equal portions.
5. Using a rolling pin or pasta machine, roll the dough very thinly and evenly to about ⅛-inch thickness. Transfer to a lightly floured peel, brush with olive oil, and scatter the za'atar evenly over the surface (if using). Gently press the spice into the dough using your fingertips.
6. Bake directly on the floor of your medium-hot wood-fired oven until blistered and colored but not totally crisp, 2 to 3 minutes. Enjoy immediately.

ROSEMARY FOCACCIA

MAKES ONE 12-BY-16-INCH FOCACCIA
Prep time: 2 hours
Cook time: 20 to 30 minutes

Ingredients

FOR THE SPONGE
- 1½ cups lukewarm water
- 2 tablespoons plus 2 teaspoons active dry yeast

- ½ cup extra-virgin olive oil

FOR THE DOUGH
- 16 ounces (3½ cups) bread flour
- 9¼ ounces (2 cups) semolina flour
- 1 tablespoon kosher salt
- ¼ cup extra-virgin olive oil
- ½ cup fresh rosemary leaves
- 2 tablespoons sea salt flakes

DIRECTIONS

TO MAKE THE SPONGE

1. Put the warm water in the work bowl of a stand mixer and sprinkle the yeast evenly over the surface. Stir to dissolve. Add the olive oil and mix by hand. Set the work bowl in a warm location.
2. After 20 to 30 minutes, you should notice small bubbles beginning to form on the surface of the sponge and a pleasant "bready-yeasty" smell beginning to arise.

TO MAKE THE DOUGH

1. Line a half sheet pan with parchment paper.
2. In a large bowl, combine the bread and semolina flours and the salt.
3. Attach the dough hook to your mixer. Mix the sponge on medium-low speed. Gradually add the flour mixture, a cup at a time, allowing the flours to be absorbed into the wet mixture before adding more. Mix thoroughly for 5 minutes, making sure no dry **ingredients** remain.
4. Using a spatula, scrape out the dough directly onto the prepared sheet pan and gently spread out the dough. Don't worry if it doesn't fully cover the parchment. Allow the dough to rest, uncovered, in a warm spot for 20 minutes.
5. Using your fingers, spread the dough a bit more evenly into the pan, trying to take the dough all the way to the edges. Allow the dough to rest for another 20 minutes and then repeat until the entire sheet tray is covered evenly with the focaccia dough. Allow to rest a final time until the dough has risen and filled the sheet tray completely, another 20 to 30 minutes.
6. You are now ready to top the focaccia. Dip your fingertips in the olive oil and press them into the dough to make shallow dimples all over the surface. Repeat until the entire sheet pan is pockmarked and oily.
7. Mix the rosemary with the remaining olive oil. Dot the surface with the herbs, pressing them gently into the dough, and drizzle any remaining oil over the focaccia. Scatter the salt flakes evenly over the surface. The focaccia is now ready for the oven.

TO BAKE THE FOCACCIA

1. In your wood-fired oven, allow a medium-hot fire to burn down so it is no longer flaming. You should have a nice mass of glowing embers and a fully heated oven. If you have a laser thermometer, you are looking for a floor temperature of around 425°F.
2. Insert the sheet tray opposite the fire source and bake until the focaccia is puffed and deep

golden. I like to rotate the pan frequently; this allows me to check the progress of the bake and also gauge the fire's intensity. If it's too cool, I add a small piece of wood; too hot and I can cover the dough loosely with a piece of heavy aluminum foil to slow the browning on the surface.

3. Approximately 20 minutes of baking should set the dough but, depending on your fire, it may take another 10 minutes. Remove the pan from the oven and allow it to cool slightly.

4. With a sharp knife, cut around the edges of the dough and release it from the pan in one slab. The parchment paper should still be on the baked focaccia, but if it isn't, don't fret.

5. Slide the dough back onto the warm oven floor for a final bake. This ensures a nice, evenly crispy crust.

6. Transfer to a cooling rack. When cool, invert and peel off the parchment paper. Cut into rectangular "fingers" and serve.

SWEET DOUGH FOR HAND PIES

MAKES TWO 6-INCH PIES
Prep time: 30 to 40 minutes

Ingredients

- 4½ ounces (1 cup) all-purpose flour
- 4½ ounces (1 cup) 00 flour
- 1 teaspoon sugar
- ¼ teaspoon kosher salt
- ¾ cup (1½ sticks) very cold unsalted butter, cut into 12 equal cubes, divided
- ½ cup ice water

DIRECTIONS

1. In the bowl of a stand mixer fitted with the paddle attachment, mix the two flours, sugar, and salt just to combine.

2. Add 8 of the butter cubes and mix on low speed until the butter begins to break down and the mixture has a sandy appearance. Stop the mixer and sort through the unformed dough by hand, using your fingers to pinch together any large chunks of butter that remain. Mix on low for 2 or 4 more turns. Add the remaining 4 butter cubes and again mix on low until the butter is slightly incorporated, about 2 minutes. Stop the mixer and remove the work bowl. Repeat the pinching step and make sure there are no remaining large chunks of butter in the mixture.

3. Make a well in the center of the shaggy mass. Add the ice water to the well and gently cover the water pool with the surrounding dough crumbs. Let the dough stand for 5 minutes to allow it to absorb some of the water.

4. Mix the dough by hand, quickly and evenly. Knead the dough only long enough so it forms a moist, slightly sticky ball, being careful not to overwork it.

5. Divide the dough into two equal portions and wrap each in plastic wrap. Flatten each ball into

a smooth disc about ½ inch thick. The dough should have a nice, even marbled appearance, streaked with butter.

6. Refrigerate the dough until ready to use, at least 2 hours and up to 24 hours.

ESSENTIAL GARLIC OIL

MAKES ABOUT 1½ CUPS

Prep time: 15 minutes

Ingredients

- 1 bunch spring garlic (4 or 5 shoots), green tops included, or 8 garlic cloves, peeled
- 1 cup extra-virgin olive oil

DIRECTIONS

1. If you are using garlic shoots, peel away the outer layer to reveal the pale inner layer. Slice off the root end and discard, then split the garlic shoots in half lengthwise.

2. Line up the split garlic shoots and slice crosswise into crescents 1/16 inch thick. Slice the entire white portion and a good deal of the green tops. You should have about ½ cup sliced garlic in total.

3. If you are using garlic cloves, cut them in half and then cut out the bitter germ that runs down the center, and discard it. Slice the cloves thinly, then chop very finely.

4. Transfer the garlic to a small bowl and cover with the oil.

SIMPLE TOMATO SAUCE

MAKES ABOUT 2 CUPS

Prep time: 5 minutes

Ingredients

- 1 (28-ounce) can whole peeled tomatoes
- ¼ cup extra-virgin olive oil
- 3 or 4 fresh basil leaves
- 2 teaspoons salt

DIRECTIONS

1. This could not be simpler. Open the can of tomatoes and add the oil, basil leaves, and salt. Using the wand of an immersion blender, purée until smooth. Or, transfer the **ingredients** to a countertop blender or food processor and purée until well incorporated.

2. Taste and adjust the seasoning with salt or olive oil.

OVEN-ROASTED RED SAUCE

MAKES ABOUT 2½ CUPS
Prep time: 10 minutes Cook time: 20 minutes

Ingredients

- 2 fresh basil sprigs
- ½ yellow onion, thinly sliced
- 3 pounds ripe organic tomatoes, such as Early Girl or Roma, cored
- ¼ to ½ cup extra-virgin olive oil
- 1 tablespoon salt

DIRECTIONS

1. Line the bottom of the gratin dish with the basil sprigs, followed by the onion slices, and finally the tomatoes, cored-side down. Drizzle the entire dish with the olive oil so the vegetables are well coated, and sprinkle the salt over all.
2. Build a nice hot fire with a generous bed of coals. Place the gratin dish directly next to the active coal bed, as close to the fire as possible, but not in the embers. Select a small piece of wood and add it to the fire to create some extra heat and a bit of smoke as the wood catches.
3. Roast the tomatoes until they are noticeably charred, bubbling, and somewhat collapsed, about 20 minutes. Halfway through, move the dish to the middle of the oven so the tomatoes cook a bit more slowly.
4. Remove the gratin dish and allow it to cool slightly. Transfer the entire contents to a food mill and pass it through. The basil stems, tomato skins, and most of the seeds will be left behind, and you will have a thin purée. If you prefer, return the purée to the gratin dish and reduce further in the oven for a more concentrated sauce.
5. The sauce will keep in an airtight container in the refrigerator for up to 1 week or in the freezer for up to 2 months.

CHARRED SWEET PEPPER AND TOMATO SAUCE

MAKES ABOUT 2 CUPS
Prep time: 25 minutes
Cook time: 20 to 30 minutes

Ingredients

- 3 large red bell peppers, or a mixture of sweet red peppers

- 2 pounds very ripe organic tomatoes, halved, seeded, and diced
- 2 teaspoons salt
- 4 tablespoons extra-virgin olive oil, divided
- 1 teaspoon smoked paprika
- ½ teaspoon chili flakes
- 2 tablespoons unsalted butter, at room temperature

DIRECTIONS

1. Build a very hot fire in the wood oven and allow it to burn down to create an environment in the range of 600° to 700°F.

2. Put the whole peppers in a cast iron skillet and roast in the oven, turning frequently, until the skins are entirely blackened, 10 to 15 minutes. Remove the peppers from the oven, transfer to a bowl, cover with a kitchen towel, and allow to steam for 15 minutes.

3. Meanwhile, line a cazuela with the diced tomatoes, in a 1-inch layer. Season with salt and drizzle with 1 tablespoon of olive oil. Roast in the hottest part of the oven until slightly charred and concentrated, 10 to 15 minutes, stirring occasionally to ensure even colorization. The idea is to expose the surface area of the tomatoes to the intense heat, evaporate the tomato water, and char the flesh. Remove from the oven.

4. When the peppers are cool enough to handle, peel and seed them, reserving the flesh.

5. In a blender or food processor, combine the roasted tomatoes and peppers, paprika, chili flakes, and butter, and purée until smooth. Thin the mixture with as much of the remaining 3 tablespoons of olive oil as necessary. Strain the purée through a fine-mesh strainer to capture any tomato and pepper skins that may remain. Adjust the seasoning with salt, if necessary.

6. The sauce will keep in an airtight container in the refrigerator for up to 1 week or in the freezer for up to 2 months.

BASIC PESTO

MAKES ABOUT 2 CUPS
Prep time: 10 minutes

Ingredients

- 1 garlic clove
- Salt
- 2 tablespoons raw pine nuts
- 3 cups densely packed small, fresh basil leaves
- ¼ cup grated pecorino romano
- 1 cup extra-virgin olive oil

DIRECTIONS

1. Mash the garlic with a small pinch of salt. Add the pine nuts and mash or process to a fine paste. Gradually add small handfuls of the basil to the garlicnut paste and pound until smooth.

Continue in this manner, adding basil and pounding until a smooth green paste is achieved and you have used all the basil.

2. Transfer to a small bowl and stir in the grated cheese and just enough olive oil to create a thick, herby sauce. Season with salt.

3. This sauce can be stored in an airtight container in the refrigerator for up to 2 days but is never better than when it is freshly made.

SALSA BIANCA

MAKES ABOUT 2 CUPS
Prep time: 5 minutes
Cook time: 10 minutes

Ingredients

- 2½ cups whole milk
- 1 bay leaf
- 2 tablespoons unsalted butter
- 3 tablespoons all-purpose flour
- 1 cup grated Parmesan cheese
- ½ teaspoon salt
- 2 teaspoons chopped fresh thyme (optional)

DIRECTIONS

1. In a small saucepan, warm the whole milk with the bay leaf over a low flame and set aside.

2. In a stainless steel saucepan, melt the butter over a medium-low flame. When it begins to foam, add the flour all at once and whisk to avoid lumps. Cook the flour and butter mixture for 2 minutes, whisking constantly. If it begins to color, lower the flame.

3. Whisk in 1 cup of the warm milk and the bay leaf in a steady stream, making sure to thoroughly whisk the bottom of the pot to prevent scorching. Whisk in the remaining milk and lower the heat. Cook on a low simmer for 10 minutes, stirring occasionally to prevent lumps from forming. Remove from the heat, discard the bay leaf, and pass the milk mixture through a fine-mesh strainer into a bowl. Add the grated cheese, salt, and thyme, if using.

4. The sauce will thicken as it cools. Thin with a few teaspoons of milk to facilitate lining pizzas and calzones.

SALSA VERDE

MAKES ABOUT 1½ CUPS
Prep time: 20 minutes

Ingredients

- 1 cup finely chopped fresh flat-leaf parsley
- 2 tablespoons finely chopped fresh chives
- 2 tablespoons finely chopped chervil (optional)
- 1 tablespoon finely chopped fresh marjoram or oregano
- 1 tablespoon finely chopped fresh tarragon
- 1 shallot, minced
- 1 garlic clove, mashed to a paste
- 1 whole salt-packed anchovy, rinsed, soaked, filleted (see Prep Tip here), and finely chopped
- 2 teaspoons salt-packed capers, soaked in water for 10 minutes, drained, and roughly chopped
- Extra-virgin olive oil
- Salt
- Freshly ground black pepper
- Splash of white wine vinegar

DIRECTIONS

1. In a medium bowl, combine the parsley, chives, chervil (if using), marjoram, and tarragon. Add the shallot, garlic, anchovy, and capers.
2. Cover with enough olive oil to make a thick, herby sauce. Season with salt and a few grinds of pepper.
3. Just before you intend to serve the salsa, add a few drops of white wine vinegar. Taste and adjust the seasoning.

WILD FENNEL SAUCE

MAKES ABOUT 1 CUP
Prep time: 15 minutes

Ingredients

- ½ cup finely chopped wild fennel fronds
- 1 tablespoon finely chopped wild fennel flowers
- 1 teaspoon wild fennel seed
- Cayenne pepper
- Salt
- 1 cup extra-virgin olive oil
- 2 garlic cloves

DIRECTIONS

1. Combine the chopped fennel fronds and flowers in a bowl.
2. In a small sauté pan over low heat, lightly toast the fennel seeds. Transfer the seeds to a mortar and pestle or a spice grinder and pulverize.

3. Add the pulverized seeds to the chopped fronds and flowers. Add a small pinch of cayenne and a generous pinch of salt. Stir in the olive oil.

4. Pound the garlic cloves to a paste in the mortar and pestle and stir the paste into the fennel sauce.

5. Allow the sauce to sit at room temperature for 30 minutes for the flavors to blend. Taste and adjust with more toasted fennel seed or salt, if needed.

TAPENADE

MAKES ABOUT 2 CUPS

Prep time: 15 minutes

Ingredients

- 1½ cups pitted, chopped niçoise olives
- 2 tablespoons salt-packed capers, rinsed, soaked, and chopped
- 1 shallot, minced
- 2 garlic cloves, mashed
- 1 whole salt-packed anchovy, rinsed, soaked, filleted (see Prep Tip), and minced (optional)
- 1 tablespoon chopped fresh flat-leaf parsley
- 2 teaspoons chopped fresh marjoram
- 1 lemon
- 1 orange
- Extra-virgin olive oil

DIRECTIONS

1. In a large bowl, combine the chopped olives, capers, shallot, mashed garlic, and anchovy, if using.

2. Add the parsley and marjoram. Using a Microplane, grate the citrus zest directly over the mixture to capture the oils in the zest.

3. Stir in just enough olive oil to make a thick, herby, slightly liquid sauce. Let stand at room temperature for 30 minutes to allow the flavors to marry.

4. The tapenade will keep for up to 1 week in an airtight container in the refrigerator.

AIOLI

MAKES ABOUT 1¼ CUPS

Prep time: 15 minutes

Ingredients

- 1 extra-large egg yolk

- 1 teaspoon water
- 1 cup extra-virgin olive oil
- Juice of ¼ lemon
- Salt
- 2 garlic cloves

DIRECTIONS

1. In a small bowl, whisk together the egg yolk and water, then begin drizzling in the olive oil while constantly whisking. As the mixture begins to emulsify, continue to add the oil in a thin, steady stream, whisking the entire time.

2. If the mixture becomes too thick, add a squeeze of fresh lemon juice to thin it out, then return to adding the oil and whisking. After all the oil has been incorporated, season with salt.

3. In a mortar and pestle, mash the garlic to a fine paste with a few grains of salt.

4. Add the mashed garlic to the aïoli and set aside at room temperature for 10 minutes to allow the flavors to marry. It should resemble softly whipped cream at this stage.

5. The aïoli can be stored in the refrigerator until ready to use. Add a few drops of water or lemon juice to thin the mixture if you intend to drizzle it over a pizza.

HARISSA

MAKES ABOUT ½ CUP

Prep time: 15 minutes

Ingredients

- 1 teaspoon cumin seeds
- 1 teaspoon coriander seeds
- 1 teaspoon caraway seeds
- ½ ounce dried mild chiles, stemmed and seeded
- 1 tablespoon smoked paprika
- ½ teaspoon salt
- ⅛ teaspoon cayenne pepper
- 1 garlic clove
- 1 teaspoon tomato paste
- ⅓ cup extra-virgin olive oil
- Splash of red wine vinegar

DIRECTIONS

1. In a small skillet over medium-low heat, toast the cumin, coriander, and caraway seeds until fragrant, tossing frequently so they don't burn, about 3 minutes total. Transfer to a spice grinder or mortar and pestle and grind to a fine powder. Transfer to a small bowl.

2. Add the dried chiles to the spice grinder and process to a fine powder. Add to the ground seed mixture. Add the smoked paprika, salt, and cayenne.

3. Pound the garlic clove to a paste in a mortar and pestle and add to the dry spices, along with the tomato paste, olive oil, and vinegar. Gently stir with a whisk to evenly blend.

4. Transfer to a small jar and cover tightly. The condiment will keep for up to 3 days in the refrigerator.

ANCHOIADE
FIG AND ANCHOVY PASTE

MAKES ABOUT 1 CUP
Prep time: 10 minutes

Ingredients

- 4 garlic cloves, sliced
- 10 whole salt-packed anchovies, rinsed, soaked, and filleted (see Prep Tip here)
- 6 fresh, ripe black Mission figs, stemmed and quartered
- 1 tablespoon unsalted butter, at room temperature
- 2 teaspoons red wine vinegar
- Freshly ground black pepper
- ⅔ cup extra-virgin olive oil

DIRECTIONS

1. In a food processor, with the motor running, drop the garlic cloves and anchovy fillets down the feed tube and chop very finely. Stop the machine once and scrape down the sides of the work bowl. Add the quartered figs and process until chopped and chunky. Add the butter, red wine vinegar, season with pepper, and process for 10 seconds longer.

2. Scrape the purée into a bowl and stir in enough olive oil to make a thick, spreadable paste. Let stand at room temperature for 30 minutes for the flavors to marry. Store in an airtight container in the refrigerator for up to 3 days.

NUMBER ONE PEPPERONI AND CHEESE PIZZA

MAKES ONE 10-INCH PIZZA
Prep time: 10 minutes
Cook time: 3 to 5 minutes

Ingredients

- 1 portion Basic Go-To Easy Pizza Dough

- 2 tablespoons Essential Garlic Oil plus more for finishing
- ½ cup Oven-Roasted Red Sauce
- ½ cup shredded part-skim mozzarella
- Salt
- 2 ounces highest-quality pepperoni, thinly sliced
- Parmesan cheese

DIRECTIONS

1. Following the directions for a fully prepped oven, make sure your fire is at the desired cooking temperature with a roiling flame and a brushed and cleaned oven floor. You are now ready to make a pizza.
2. Stretch out the dough as shown in "How to Shape a Pizza" .Lightly dust your pizza peel with flour. Place your stretched dough directly on the peel and proceed to build the pizza.
3. Brush the stretched dough with the garlic oil and spread the oven-roasted tomato sauce evenly over the dough, leaving a ½-inch border all the way around the outside. Top the pie with the shredded mozzarella. Season the entire pie with a pinch of salt.
4. Scatter the pepperoni slices. Be generous with the pepperoni so everyone gets his or her fill in each bite.
5. Slide the pizza into the oven and bake for 3 to 5 minutes, rotating once or twice to ensure even cooking. Remove the pizza to a cutting board. Slice into 6 or 8 wedges. Grate Parmesan over the entire pie. Brush the crust edges with a quick pass of garlic oil to finish.

PIZZA WITH PROSCIUTTO CRUDO, RICOTTA, AND AGED BALSAMICO

MAKES ONE 10-INCH PIZZA
Prep time: 10 minutes
Cook time: 3 to 5 minutes

Ingredients

- ½ cup fresh ricotta
- Salt
- 1 tablespoon extra-virgin olive oil
- 1 portion Elevated Pizza Dough
- 3 tablespoons Essential Garlic Oil ,plus more for finishing
- ¼ cup Oven-Roasted Red Sauce
- ½ cup arugula
- 4 slices prosciutto crudo
- Freshly ground black pepper
- 1 teaspoon aged balsamic vinegar

DIRECTIONS

1. In a small bowl, whisk the ricotta to smooth the curds. Season with a pinch of salt and stir in the olive oil.
2. Following the directions for a fully prepped oven, make sure your fire is at the desired cooking temperature with a roiling flame and a brushed and cleaned oven floor. You are now ready to make a pizza.
3. Stretch out the dough as shown in "How to Shape a Pizza" .Lightly dust your pizza peel with flour. Place your stretched dough directly on the peel and proceed to build the pizza.
4. Brush the stretched dough with the garlic oil and spread the whisked ricotta evenly over the dough, leaving a ½-inch border all the way around the outside. Top the ricotta with the red sauce, followed by the arugula. Season the entire pie with a pinch of salt.
5. Slide the pizza into the oven and bake for 3 to 5 minutes, rotating once or twice to ensure even cooking. Remove the pizza to a cutting board.
6. Drape the prosciutto slices over the cooked pizza and add a few grinds of black pepper. Drizzle the entire pie with the aged balsamico . Slice into 6 or 8 wedges. Brush the crust edges with a quick pass of garlic oil to finish.

PIZZA WITH PROSCIUTTO COTTO AND GORGONZOLA

MAKES ONE 10-INCH PIZZA
Prep time: 10 minutes
Cook time: 3 to 5 minutes

Ingredients

- 1 portion Elevated Pizza Dough
- 3 tablespoons Essential Garlic Oil ,plus more for finishing
- ½ cup Salsa Bianca
- 3 ounces prosciutto cotto, thinly sliced
- ¼ cup crumbled Gorgonzola
- Salt
- 2 tablespoons chopped fresh flat-leaf parsley
- ½ teaspoon freshly squeezed lemon juice
- ½ teaspoon extra-virgin olive oil
- Freshly ground black pepper

DIRECTIONS

1. Following the directions for a fully prepped oven, make sure your fire is at the desired cooking temperature with a roiling flame and a brushed and cleaned oven floor. You are now ready to make a pizza.
2. Stretch out the dough as shown in "How to Shape a Pizza" (here). Lightly dust your pizza peel

with flour. Place your stretched dough directly on the peel and proceed to build the pizza.

3. Brush the stretched dough with the garlic oil and spread the salsa bianca evenly over the dough, leaving a ½-inch border all the way around the outside. Top the pie with the prosciutto slices and crumble on the Gorgonzola. Season the entire pie with a pinch of salt.
4. Slide the pizza into the oven and bake for 3 to 5 minutes, rotating once or twice to ensure even cooking. Remove the pizza to a cutting board.
5. Toss the parsley leaves with a squeeze of lemon juice and a few drops of olive oil, add a few grinds of black pepper, and scatter over the pie. Slice into 6 or 8 wedges. Brush the crust edges with a quick pass of garlic oil to finish.

PANCETTA PIZZA WITH SWISS CHARD AND ONIONS

MAKES ONE 10-INCH PIZZA
Prep time: 20 minutes
Cook time: 20 to 25 minutes

Ingredients

- 1 yellow onion, diced
- 1 bunch Swiss chard, leaves stripped from stems, stems reserved (optional)
- 2 tablespoons extra-virgin olive oil, divided
- Salt
- 1 portion Basic Go-To Easy Pizza Dough
- 3 tablespoons Essential Garlic Oil ,plus more for finishing
- ½ cup Simple Tomato Sauce
- ½ cup shredded Gruyère cheese
- 4 thin slices pancetta
- Freshly ground black pepper

DIRECTIONS

1. Following the directions for a fully prepped oven, make sure your fire is at the desired cooking temperature with a roiling flame and a brushed and cleaned oven floor. You are now ready to make a pizza.
2. Combine the yellow onion dice with the chard stems, if using, in a cast iron skillet, and season with 1 tablespoon of olive oil and a pinch of salt. Sauté the vegetables slowly, in the window of the oven, until tender, about 8 minutes. Set aside until ready to use.
3. Repeat with the chard leaves in the same manner, seasoning with the remaining 1 tablespoon of olive oil and a pinch of salt and sautéing slowly until wilted. Stir often to prevent burning, and add a splash of water if the pan dries out. Combine the onion-stem mixture and the cooked chard.
4. Stretch out the dough as shown in "How to Shape a Pizza" (here). Lightly dust your pizza peel

with flour. Place your stretched dough directly on the peel and proceed to build the pizza.

5. Brush the stretched dough with the garlic oil and spread the tomato sauce evenly over the dough, leaving a ½-inch border all the way around the outside. Arrange the Gruyère over the dough, followed by the greens mixture. Take care not to overload the pizza. Season the pie with a pinch of salt. Drape the pancetta slices over the pie.
6. Slide the pizza into the oven and bake for 3 to 5 minutes, rotating once or twice to ensure even cooking.
7. Remove the pizza to a cutting board and add a few grinds of black pepper. Slice into 6 or 8 wedges. Brush the crust edges with a quick pass of garlic oil to finish.

PIZZA WITH FENNEL SAUSAGE, PEPPERS, AND CALABRIAN CHILES

MAKES ONE 10-INCH PIZZA
Prep time: 20 minutes
Cook time: about 10 minutes

Ingredients

- ¾ cup thinly sliced sweet bell peppers
- 1 yellow onion, thinly sliced
- Extra-virgin olive oil
- Salt
- 4 ounces fennel sausage, casing removed, crumbled
- 1 portion Basic Go-To Easy Pizza Dough
- 2 tablespoons Essential Garlic Oil, plus more for finishing
- ¼ cup Simple Tomato Sauce
- ½ cup shredded part-skim mozzarella
- 1 tablespoon Calabrian chile purée (see A Closer Look)
- 2 tablespoons flat-leaf Italian parsley

DIRECTIONS

1. Combine the peppers and onion in a small bowl, moisten with enough olive oil to thoroughly coat the vegetables, and season with salt. Set aside to soften slightly for 10 minutes.
2. Following the directions for a fully prepped oven, make sure your fire is at the desired cooking temperature with a roiling flame and a brushed and cleaned oven floor.
3. Place the crumbled fennel sausage in a cast iron skillet and brown in the oven, about 5 minutes. Remove from the pan and drain the fat.
4. Stretch out the dough as shown in "How to Shape a Pizza" (here). Lightly dust your pizza peel with flour. Place your stretched dough directly on the peel and proceed to build the pizza.
5. Brush the stretched dough with the garlic oil and spread the tomato sauce evenly over the dough, leaving a ½-inch border all the way around the outside. Top the pie with the

mozzarella cheese. Season the entire pie with a pinch of salt.
6. Lift the peppers and onions from the bowl and allow any excess liquid to drain off. Spread evenly over the pizza. Arrange the crumbled sausage over the pie.
7. Slide the pizza into the oven and bake for 3 to 5 minutes, rotating once or twice to ensure even cooking. Remove the pizza to a cutting board. Slice into 6 or 8 wedges.
8. In a thin drizzle, garnish the cooked pizza with the Calabrian chile purée. Brush the crust edges with a quick pass of garlic oil to finish. Garnish with the parsley leaves.

FOUR SEASONS PIZZA

MAKES ONE 6-BY-12-INCH PIZZA
Prep time: 30 minutes
Cook time: about 10 minutes

Ingredients

- ½ cup wild mushrooms such as black trumpets or chanterelles
- Extra-virgin olive oil
- Salt
- 1 portion Basic Go-To Easy Pizza Dough
- 1 tablespoon Essential Garlic Oil, plus more for finishing
- ¾ cup Simple Tomato Sauce
- ¼ cup Basic Pesto
- ¾ cup shredded part-skim mozzarella
- 2 fresh basil leaves
- 2 whole salt-packed anchovy fillets, rinsed, soaked, filleted (see Prep Tip here), and halved lengthwise (8 pieces total)
- 2 ounces smoked ham, thinly sliced
- 1 ounce crumbled Gorgonzola
- Parmesan cheese
- Freshly ground black pepper

DIRECTIONS
1. Toss the mushrooms with a little olive oil and salt and roast them in a cazuela in the oven until they are wilted and slightly caramelized, about 7 minutes. Set aside to cool.
2. Following the directions for a fully prepped oven, make sure your fire is at the desired cooking temperature with a roiling flame and a brushed and cleaned oven floor. You are now ready to make a pizza.
3. Stretch out the dough as shown in "How to Shape a Pizza" (here). Lightly dust your pizza peel with flour. Place your stretched dough directly on the peel and proceed to build the pizza.
4. Brush the stretched dough with the garlic oil and spread the tomato sauce evenly over three-quarters of the dough, leaving a ½-inch border. Spread the pesto over the last quarter of the dough. Arrange the shredded mozzarella over the entire pie. Garnish the pesto portion with

the basil leaves. Garnish another quarter with the anchovy fillets, and another with the cooked wild mushrooms. For the last quarter, lay down the ham slices and dot with the Gorgonzola. You should have four distinct sections.
5. Slide the pizza into the oven and bake for 3 to 5 minutes, rotating once or twice to ensure even cooking. Remove the pizza to a cutting board, grate Parmesan over the entire pie, and add a few grinds of black pepper. Slice into four quarters and those quarters into bite-size pieces for all to enjoy. Brush the crust edges with a quick pass of garlic oil to finish.

SALAMI PIZZA WITH PARSLEY-PARMESAN SALAD

MAKES ONE 10-INCH PIZZA
Prep time: 10 minutes
Cook time: 3 to 5 minutes

Ingredients

- 1 portion Basic Go-To Easy Pizza Dough
- 3 tablespoons Essential Garlic Oil, plus more for finishing
- ½ cup Oven-Roasted Red Sauce
- ½ cup shredded part-skim mozzarella
- 10 thin slices imported dry salami, preferably Tuscan-style
- ½ cup fresh flat-leaf parsley leaves
- ¼ cup shredded Parmesan cheese
- Salt
- Extra-virgin olive oil

DIRECTIONS

1. Following the directions for a fully prepped oven, make sure your fire is at the desired cooking temperature with a roiling flame and a brushed and cleaned oven floor. You are now ready to make a pizza.
2. Stretch out the dough as shown in "How to Shape a Pizza" (here). Lightly dust your pizza peel with flour. Place your stretched dough directly on the peel and proceed to build the pizza.
3. Brush the stretched dough with the garlic oil and spread the red sauce over the dough, leaving a ½-inch border. Top with the shredded mozzarella and the thinly sliced salami, covering the entire surface of the pie by overlapping the salami rounds.
4. Slide the pizza into the oven and bake for 3 to 5 minutes, rotating once or twice to ensure even cooking. Remove the pizza to a cutting board and cut into 6 to 8 wedges. Brush the crust edges with a quick pass of garlic oil to finish.
5. In a small bowl, toss the parsley and Parmesan together, then dress with a pinch of salt and a few drops of olive oil. Mound the parsley salad in the center of the pizza and encourage guests to get a bit of green with every slice they enjoy.

FENNEL SAUSAGE AND WILTED GREENS PIZZA WITH FRESH MOZZARELLA

MAKES ONE 10-INCH PIZZA
Prep time: 20 minutes
Cook time: 25 minutes

Ingredients

- 1 yellow onion, diced
- 1 bunch Swiss chard, leaves stripped from stems, stems reserved (optional)
- 2 tablespoons extra-virgin olive oil, divided
- Salt
- 4 ounces fennel sausage, casing removed, crumbled
- 1 portion Whole-Wheat Pizza Dough
- 2 tablespoons Essential Garlic Oil, plus more for finishing
- ¼ cup Simple Tomato Sauce
- 4 ounces buffalo mozzarella, thinly sliced

DIRECTIONS

1. Following the directions for a fully prepped oven, make sure your fire is at the desired cooking temperature with a roiling flame and a brushed and cleaned oven floor. You are now ready to make a pizza.
2. Combine the yellow onion dice with the chard stems, if using, in a cast iron skillet, and season with 1 tablespoon of olive oil and a pinch of salt. Sauté the vegetables slowly, in the window of the oven, until tender, about 8 minutes. Set aside until ready to use.
3. Repeat with the chard leaves in the same manner, seasoning and sautéing slowly until wilted. Stir often to prevent burning and add a splash of water if the pan dries out. Combine the onion-stem mixture and the cooked chard.
4. Place the crumbled fennel sausage in a cast iron skillet and brown in the oven, about 5 minutes. Remove from the pan and drain the fat.
5. Stretch out the dough as shown in "How to Shape a Pizza". Lightly dust your pizza peel with flour. Place your stretched dough directly on the peel and proceed to build the pizza.
6. Brush the stretched dough with the garlic oil and spread the tomato sauce evenly over the dough, leaving a ½-inch border all the way around the outside. Top the pie with the vegetable mixture and the sliced mozzarella cheese. Season the entire pie with a pinch of salt. Arrange the crumbled sausage over the greens and cheese.
7. Slide the pizza into the oven and bake for 3 to 5 minutes, rotating once or twice to ensure even cooking. Remove the pizza to a cutting board. Slice into 6 or 8 wedges. Brush the crust edges

with a quick pass of garlic oil to finish.

WHOLE-WHEAT PIZZA WITH PANCETTA, POTATO, AND ASPARAGUS

MAKES TWO 6-INCH PIZZAS
Prep time: 30 minutes
Cook time: about 10 minutes per pizza

Ingredients

- 8 ounces Yellow Finn potatoes, sliced ⅛ inch thick
- Salt
- Extra-virgin olive oil
- 2 thick asparagus spears
- 1 portion Whole-Wheat Pizza Dough ,divided into two equal balls
- 2 tablespoons Essential Garlic Oil ,plus more for finishing
- ½ cup Salsa Bianca
- ½ cup shredded Fontina cheese
- 6 ounces pancetta, thinly sliced
- Parmesan cheese
- Freshly ground black pepper

DIRECTIONS
1. Following the directions for a fully prepped oven, make sure your fire is at the desired cooking temperature with a roiling flame and a brushed and cleaned oven floor.
2. In a bowl, toss the potato slices with a generous pinch of salt and moisten with a splash each of olive oil and water. Arrange the potatoes in a single layer on an unlined half sheet pan and roast in a very hot oven until they begin to take on color and soften, 4 to 7 minutes. Allow the potatoes to cool completely, taste, and adjust the seasoning with more salt if needed. Set aside until you're ready to build the pizza.
3. Prepare the asparagus by snapping off the woody stems and discarding. Using a mandoline, carefully slice the raw asparagus lengthwise, creating paper-thin ribbons. Toss the asparagus ribbons in a small bowl with a splash of oil and a pinch of salt.
4. Stretch out one piece of dough as shown in "How to Shape a Pizza" (here). Lightly dust your pizza peel with flour. Place your stretched dough directly on the peel and proceed to build the pizza.
5. Brush the stretched dough with the garlic oil and spread half of the salsa bianca over the pizza. Distribute half of the shredded Fontina evenly over the dough, leaving a ½-inch border all the way around the outside. Add half of the cooked potato slices and half of the asparagus to the pie. Season with a pinch of salt. Top with half of the pancetta.
6. Slide the pizza into the oven and bake for 3 to 5 minutes, rotating once or twice to ensure even

cooking. Remove the pizza to a cutting board, grate Parmesan cheese over the entire pie, and add a few grinds of black pepper. Slice into 4 wedges. Brush the crust edges with a quick pass of garlic oil to finish.
7. Repeat with the second pizza.

APPLEWOOD SMOKED BACON AND SUNNY-SIDE UP EGGS WITH PARMESAN

MAKES ONE 10-INCH PIZZA
Prep time: 10 minutes
Cook time: 5 to 7 minutes

Ingredients

- 1 portion Whole-Wheat Pizza Dough
- 1 tablespoon Essential Garlic Oil ,plus more for finishing
- ½ cup Salsa Bianca
- ¼ cup shredded part-skim mozzarella
- ½ cup thinly sliced red onion
- 4 ounces uncooked thinly sliced applewood smoked bacon or precooked thicker bacon
- 2 eggs
- Salt
- Parmesan cheese
- Freshly ground black pepper

DIRECTIONS

1. Following the directions for a fully prepped oven, make sure your fire is at the desired cooking temperature with a roiling flame and a brushed and cleaned oven floor. You are now ready to make a pizza.
2. Stretch out the dough as shown in "How to Shape a Pizza" (here). Lightly dust your pizza peel with flour. Place your stretched dough directly on the peel and proceed to build the pizza.
3. Brush the stretched dough with the garlic oil and spread the salsa bianca over the dough, leaving a ½-inch border. Top with the shredded mozzarella and the thinly sliced onion, followed by the uncooked bacon (if using).
4. Slide the pizza into the oven and bake for 2 minutes to set the bottom of the pie. Remove from the oven and crack the eggs carefully onto the pizza. Season the eggs with salt. Return to the oven and cook for 3 to 5 minutes longer, rotating once or twice to ensure even cooking. Remove the pizza to a cutting board when the bacon has cooked through and the egg whites are set but the yolks remain soft.
5. Grate Parmesan cheese over the entire pie and add a few grinds of black pepper. Garnish with

the precooked bacon (if using). Brush the crust edges with a quick pass of the garlic oil to finish. Enjoy as a proper breakfast, with a knife and fork.

PIZZA WITH CHORIZO Y PAPAS, FRESH CILANTRO, AND LIME

MAKES ONE 10-INCH PIZZA
Prep time: 40 minutes
Cook time: 30 minutes

Ingredients

- 1 russet potato, peeled and cut into ½-inch dice
- 4 ounces Mexican-style chorizo, crumbled
- 1 portion Basic Go-To Easy Pizza Dough (here) or Spelt Pizza Dough (here)
- 2 ounces Cotija cheese, crumbled
- 2 tablespoons crème fraîche
- ¼ cup chopped fresh cilantro leaves and stems
- 1 lime

DIRECTIONS

1. Cook the potato in boiling salted water until tender, about 10 minutes. Drain well and reserve.
2. Preheat a cast iron skillet for 5 minutes in the wood oven, add the chorizo, and cook in a medium-hot environment for 3 minutes to render some of the fat. Add the cooked potato to the skillet, stir to combine, and return to the oven. Continue to cook until the chorizo is cooked through and the potatoes receive some color, about 3 minutes more. Remove and set aside to cool completely.
3. Following the directions for a fully prepped oven, make sure your fire is at the desired cooking temperature with a roiling flame and a brushed and cleaned oven floor. You are now ready to make a pizza.
4. Stretch out the dough as shown in "How to Shape a Pizza" (here). Lightly dust your pizza peel with flour. Place your stretched dough directly on the peel and proceed to build the pizza.
5. Spread the chorizo and potato mixture over the stretched pizza crust in a thin, even layer, leaving a ½-inch border around the pizza. Top with the crumbled Cotija cheese.
6. Slide the pizza into the oven and bake for 3 to 5 minutes, rotating once or twice to ensure even cooking. Remove the pizza to a cutting board, drizzle the crème fraîche over the pie, garnish with the fresh cilantro, and squeeze a bit of lime juice over it all. Slice into 6 or 8 wedges.

PIZZA WITH LAMB SAUSAGE, CARAMELIZED ONIONS, AND MARJORAM

MAKES ONE 10-INCH PIZZA
Prep time: 35 minutes
Cook time: 30 minutes

Ingredients

- 2 yellow onions, thinly sliced
- 2 tablespoons extra-virgin olive oil
- Salt
- 4 ounces lamb sausage
- 1 portion Elevated Pizza Dough (here)
- 1 tablespoon Essential Garlic Oil (here), plus more for finishing
- ½ cup Charred Sweet Pepper and Tomato Sauce (here)
- ½ cup shredded part-skim mozzarella
- Freshly ground black pepper
- 2 tablespoons roughly chopped fresh marjoram

DIRECTIONS

1. Following the directions for a fully prepped oven, make sure your fire is at the desired cooking temperature, with a roiling flame and a brushed and cleaned oven floor.
2. Toss the onion slices with the olive oil and salt in a cazuela and roast slowly in the mouth of the oven, tossing frequently. Prevent the onions from burning by adding a splash of water if needed. The onions will lose considerable volume, begin to color slightly, and become much sweeter. When the onions have deeply colored and lost most of their volume, after 20 minutes or so, remove the pan. Allow to cool.
3. Meanwhile, remove the sausage from its casing and crumble into a cast iron skillet. Roast in the oven until the fat begins to render and the meat colors slightly, 3 to 4 minutes. Remove from the skillet, drain the fat, and set aside.
4. Stretch out the dough as shown in "How to Shape a Pizza" (here). Lightly dust your pizza peel with flour. Place your stretched dough directly on the peel and proceed to build the pizza.
5. Brush the stretched dough with the garlic oil and spread the pepper and tomato sauce evenly over the dough, leaving a ½-inch border all the way around the outside. Arrange the shredded cheese on top, distributing evenly.
6. Spread the caramelized onions over the cheese, crumble over the partially cooked lamb sausage, then season the entire pie with a pinch of salt.
7. Slide the pizza into the oven and bake for 3 to 5 minutes, rotating once or twice to ensure even

cooking. Remove the pizza to a cutting board and add a few grinds of black pepper. Garnish with the chopped marjoram. Slice into 6 or 8 wedges. Brush the crust edges with a quick pass of the garlic oil to finish.

ALSATIAN-STYLE TART OF STEWED ONIONS, BACON LARDONS, AND BLACK PEPPER

MAKES ONE 12-BY-18-INCH TART
Prep time: 40 minutes
Cook time: 25 minutes

Ingredients

- 4 medium yellow onions, thinly sliced
- Extra-virgin olive oil
- 1 tablespoon salt
- ¼ cup Alsatian white wine or German-style pilsner beer (optional)
- 2 portions Basic Go-To Easy Pizza Dough (here)
- 8 ounces Gruyère cheese, shredded
- 1 pound smoked bacon, cut into 1-inch lardons, rendered until slightly crispy, and drained on a paper towel
- ¼ cup crème fraîche
- 1 cup fromage blanc cheese
- Freshly ground black pepper

DIRECTIONS

1. Toss the onions with enough olive oil to moisten and season with the salt. Transfer to a cazuela large enough to hold the onions in a single layer and slowly roast in the window of the wood oven for about 15 minutes, stirring often. The idea is to soften the onions but avoid coloring them too much. Add wine, beer, or water if the edges begin to brown too quickly, or if the cazuela dries out. When sufficiently softened, remove from the oven and allow to cool.
2. Brush a half sheet pan with a small amount of olive oil and stretch the dough as outlined in the recipe for Rosemary Focaccia (here). Gradually press the dough into the corners of the pan, eventually filling in the entire rectangle. Allow the dough to rest a few minutes if you are having trouble stretching it and filling in the form.
3. Top the dough with the onions, followed by the Gruyère. Arrange the bacon lardons and press them lightly into the onion mixture. Drizzle the tart with the crème fraîche and finally top with small spoonfuls of the fromage blanc.
4. In a medium-hot oven, bake the tart, rotating often until the dough sets, the onions begin to color, and the bacon crisps. Check to see that the crust is browning nicely by lifting the

dough with a spatula. If the tart seems to be cooking too quickly, move the pan to the window where it can cook more slowly and steadily. The total cooking time should be under 10 minutes.

5. If you desire a firm, crisp crust, carefully slide the dough from the pan and finish directly on the hearth floor until crisped and browned.
6. Remove from the oven, transfer to a cutting board, and cut into equal squares. Finish with a generous grinding of black pepper.

FENNEL PIZZA WITH BRESAOLA AND LEMON

MAKES ONE 10-INCH PIZZA
Prep time: 10 minutes
Cook time: 3 to 5 minutes

Ingredients

- 1 portion Elevated Pizza Dough (here)
- ½ cup Wild Fennel Sauce (here)
- 1 cup very thinly sliced fennel bulb, divided
- Salt
- 10 thin slices bresaola
- Juice of ½ lemon
- Parmesan cheese
- Freshly ground black pepper

DIRECTIONS

1. Following the directions for a fully prepped oven, make sure your fire is at the desired cooking temperature with a roiling flame and a brushed and cleaned oven floor. You are now ready to make a pizza.
2. Stretch out the dough as shown in "How to Shape a Pizza" (here). Lightly dust your pizza peel with flour. Place your stretched dough directly on the peel and proceed to build the pizza.
3. Spread the fennel sauce generously over the dough, leaving a ½-inch border. In a small bowl, toss half of the sliced fennel with a generous pinch of salt and spread evenly over the dough.
4. Slide the pizza into the oven and bake for 3 to 5 minutes, rotating once or twice to ensure even cooking. Remove the pizza to a cutting board and garnish with the bresaola slices. Slice into 6 or 8 wedges.
5. Dress the remaining fennel slices with the lemon juice and salt, and heap on the pizza. Grate Parmesan over the entire pie and add a few grinds of black pepper.

MERGUEZ FLATBREAD WITH ZUCCHINI, SMOKY EGGPLANT, AND CILANTRO

MAKES ONE 10-INCH FLATBREAD
Prep time: 1 hour
Cook time: 3 to 5 minutes

Ingredients

- 1 portion North African Flatbread dough (here), omitting the za'atar
- ¼ cup Harissa (here)
- ½ cup very thinly sliced zucchini
- ½ recipe Eggplant Roasted in the Coals (here)
- 4 ounces merguez sausage, casing removed, crumbled
- Salt
- ¼ cup chopped fresh cilantro
- 2 tablespoons crème fraîche

DIRECTIONS

1. Following the directions for a fully prepped oven, make sure your fire is at the desired cooking temperature with a roiling flame and a brushed and cleaned oven floor. You are now ready to make a flatbread pizza.
2. Follow the instructions as outlined in the North African Flatbread recipe for shaping. Stretch out the dough as shown in "How to Shape a Pizza" (here). Lightly dust your pizza peel with flour. Place your stretched dough directly on the peel and proceed to build the pizza.
3. Brush the stretched dough with the harissa and spread out the zucchini on the pizza, leaving a ½-inch border all the way around the outside. Spread the eggplant purée in between the zucchini on the exposed dough. Dot the crumbled merguez in the remaining exposed spaces of the flatbread. Season the entire pie with a pinch of salt.
4. Slide the pizza into the oven and bake for 3 to 5 minutes, rotating once or twice to ensure even cooking. Remove the pizza to a cutting board, scatter the cilantro over the pie, and drizzle with the crème fraîche. Slice into 6 or 8 wedges.

PIZZA WITH CHICKEN SAUSAGE, RED ONIONS, AND CHARRED SWEET PEPPER AND TOMATO SAUCE

MAKES ONE 10-INCH PIZZA
Prep time: 30 minutes
Cook time: 3 to 5 minutes

Ingredients

- 1 portion Basic Go-To Easy Pizza Dough (here)
- 2 tablespoons Essential Garlic Oil (here), plus more for finishing
- ½ cup Charred Sweet Pepper and Tomato Sauce (here)
- ½ cup shredded part-skim mozzarella
- 1 red onion, thinly sliced on a mandoline
- Salt
- 1 teaspoon finely chopped fresh rosemary
- Extra-virgin olive oil
- 4 ounces chicken sausage, casing removed, crumbled
- Parmesan cheese
- Freshly ground black pepper

DIRECTIONS

1. Following the directions for a fully prepped oven, make sure your fire is at the desired cooking temperature with a roiling flame and a brushed and cleaned oven floor. You are now ready to make a pizza.
2. Stretch out the dough as shown in "How to Shape a Pizza" (here). Lightly dust your pizza peel with flour. Place your stretched dough directly on the peel and proceed to build the pizza.
3. Brush the stretched dough with the garlic oil and spread the pepper and tomato sauce evenly, leaving a ½-inch border all the way around the outside. Distribute the shredded mozzarella cheese evenly over the pizza.
4. In a small bowl, toss the sliced red onion with a pinch of salt, the chopped rosemary, and a splash of olive oil.
5. Arrange the onion-herb mixture over the cheese. Fill in the spaces with the crumbled chicken sausage. Sprinkle the entire pie with a pinch of salt.
6. Slide the pizza into the oven and bake for 3 to 5 minutes, rotating once or twice to ensure even cooking. Remove the pizza to a cutting board, grate Parmesan cheese over the entire pie, and add a few grinds of black pepper. Slice into 6 or 8 wedges. Brush the crust edges with a quick pass of the garlic oil to finish.

PIZZA WITH SAN MARZANO TOMATOES AND BRAISED CHICKEN LEGS

MAKES ONE 10-INCH PIZZA

Prep time: 20 minutes for the braise, 15 minutes for the pizza

Cook time: 1 hour 10 minutes for the braise, 3 to 5 minutes for the pizza

Ingredients

FOR THE BRAISE
- 2 organic bone-in, skin-on whole chicken legs
- Salt
- Freshly ground black pepper
- 1 carrot, peeled and cut into 1-inch pieces
- 1 medium yellow onion, cut into
- inch pieces
- 1 fennel bulb, cut into 1-inch pieces
- Extra-virgin olive oil
- 1 bay leaf
- 2 fresh thyme sprigs
- ½ teaspoon whole black peppercorns
- 1 piece lemon peel, 1 inch wide and 3 inches long
- ½ cup dry white wine
- 4 cups organic chicken stock

FOR THE PIZZA
- 1 portion Basic Go-To Easy Pizza Dough
- 2 tablespoons Essential Garlic Oil ,plus more for finishing
- ¼ cup shredded part-skim mozzarella
- 1 cup arugula
- 1 (28-ounce) can whole San Marzano tomatoes, drained
- Salt
- Parmesan cheese
- Freshly ground black pepper
- 1 recipe Tapenade

DIRECTIONS

TO MAKE THE BRAISE
1. Two days before you plan to serve the pizza, trim away the excess fat from the chicken legs and season them with salt and pepper. Cover and refrigerate overnight.
2. The next day, remove the chicken from the refrigerator and get ready to build the braise. Preheat the oven to 400°F.
3. Sauté the carrot, onion, and fennel in a bit of olive oil until softened, about 5 minutes. Season with salt. Transfer to a cazuela large enough to hold the vegetables and chicken legs snugly in a single layer. Add the bay leaf, thyme, peppercorns, and lemon peel. Nestle in the chicken legs, skin-side down, then add the wine and enough stock to almost cover the meat. Cover

tightly with aluminum foil and place in the oven.
4. After 15 minutes turn the oven down to 325°F. Cook for 30 minutes longer. Uncover the chicken, carefully turn the legs over so they're skin side up, and continue to cook until the meat is tender but not falling off the bone, about 20 minutes longer. The skin should be deeply browned and crispy.
5. Remove from the oven and let cool. Skim as much fat from the surface as possible. Discard the fat. Cover and refrigerate until ready to use.
6. The following day, remove the chicken from the refrigerator and allow it to come to room temperature. Shred the chicken meat from the bones. Chop the skin finely and mix it in with the meat. Strain the broth and use it for another purpose, such as soup. Discard the vegetables.

TO MAKE THE PIZZA
1. Following the directions for a fully prepped oven, make sure your fire is at the desired cooking temperature with a roiling flame and a brushed and cleaned oven floor. You are now ready to make a pizza.
2. Stretch out the dough as shown in "How to Shape a Pizza" (here). Lightly dust your pizza peel with flour. Place your stretched dough directly on the peel and proceed to build the pizza.
3. Brush the stretched dough with the garlic oil and spread the cheese evenly, leaving a ½-inch border all the way around the outside. Scatter the arugula over the entire pizza. Crush the tomatoes with your hands and arrange the chunky pieces on top, then fill in the spaces with the shredded chicken meat and skin. Sprinkle the entire pie with a pinch of salt.
4. Slide the pizza into the oven and bake for 3 to 5 minutes, rotating once or twice to ensure even cooking. Remove the pizza to a cutting board, grate Parmesan cheese over the pie, and add a few grinds of black pepper. Drizzle with tapenade.
5. Slice into 6 or 8 wedges. Brush the crust edges with a quick pass of the garlic oil to finish.

SHREDDED DUCK LEG AND WINTER SQUASH PIZZA WITH SCAMORZA

MAKES ONE 10-INCH PIZZA

Prep time: 20 minutes for the braise, 20 minutes for the pizza

Cook time: 1 hour 10 minutes for the braise, 3 to 5 minutes for the pizza

Ingredients

FOR THE BRAISE
- 2 organic bone-in, skin-on whole duck legs
- Salt
- Freshly ground black pepper
- 1 carrot, peeled and cut into 1-inch pieces

- 1 leek, cut into 1-inch pieces
- 1 fennel bulb, cut into 1-inch pieces
- Extra-virgin olive oil
- 1 bay leaf
- 2 fresh thyme sprigs
- ½ teaspoon whole black peppercorns
- 1 whole star anise
- 1 piece orange peel, 1 inch wide and 3 inches long
- ½ cup dry white wine
- 4 cups organic chicken stock

FOR THE PIZZA
- ½ winter squash, such as kabocha or butternut, peeled, seeded, and cut into ⅛-inch-thick slices
- 2 tablespoons Essential Garlic Oil (here), divided, plus more for finishing
- Salt
- 1 portion Elevated Pizza Dough (here)
- ½ cup shredded Scamorza cheese Parmesan cheese
- Freshly ground black pepper
- 2 tablespoons chopped fresh parsley

DIRECTIONS

TO MAKE THE BRAISE

1. Two days before you plan to serve the pizza, trim away the excess fat from the duck legs and season them with salt and pepper. Cover and refrigerate overnight.
2. The next day, remove the duck from the refrigerator and get ready to build the braise. Preheat the oven to 400°F.
3. Sauté the carrot, leek, and fennel in a bit of olive oil until softened, about 5 minutes. Season with salt. Transfer to a cazuela large enough to hold the vegetables and duck legs snugly in a single layer. Add the bay leaf, thyme, peppercorns, star anise, and orange peel. Nestle in the duck legs, skin-side down, then add the wine and enough stock to almost cover the meat. Cover tightly with aluminum foil and place in the oven.
4. After 15 minutes turn the oven down to 325°F. Cook for 30 minutes longer. Uncover the duck, carefully turn the legs over so they're skin-side up, and continue to cook until the meat is tender but not falling off the bone, about 20 minutes longer. The skin should be deeply browned and crispy.
5. Remove from the oven and let cool. Skim as much fat from the surface as possible. Discard the fat. Cover and refrigerate until ready to use.
6. The following day, remove the duck from the refrigerator and allow it to come to room temperature. Shred the duck meat from the bones. Chop the skin finely and mix it in with the meat. Strain the broth and use it for another purpose such as soup. Discard the vegetables.

TO MAKE THE PIZZA

1. Toss the squash slices in 1 tablespoon of the garlic oil and season with salt. Arrange on a half sheet pan in a single layer and roast in a medium-hot oven until tender, 4 to 5 minutes. Allow the squash to cool before building the pie.
2. Following the directions for a fully prepped oven, make sure your fire is at the desired cooking temperature with a roiling flame and a brushed and cleaned oven floor. You are now ready to make a pizza.
3. Stretch out the dough as shown in "How to Shape a Pizza" (here). Lightly dust your pizza peel with flour. Place your stretched dough directly on the peel and proceed to build the pizza.
4. Brush the stretched dough with the remaining 1 tablespoon garlic oil and spread the shredded Scamorza evenly, leaving a ½-inch border all the way around the outside. Arrange the roasted squash slices in a single layer over the pie. Fill in the spaces with the shredded duck meat and skin. Sprinkle the entire pie with a pinch of salt.
5. Slide the pizza into the oven and bake for 3 to 5 minutes, rotating once or twice to ensure even cooking. Remove the pizza to a cutting board, grate Parmesan cheese over the entire pie, and add a few grinds of black pepper. Garnish with the chopped parsley. Slice into 6 or 8 wedges. Brush the crust edges with a quick pass of the garlic oil to finish.

PIZZA WITH FRESH FIGS, CARAMELIZED ONIONS, AND ANCHOIADE

MAKES ONE 10-INCH PIZZA
Prep time: 35 minutes
Cook time: 3 to 5 minutes

Ingredients

- 1 small yellow onion, thinly sliced
- Extra-virgin olive oil
- Salt
- 1 portion Basic Go-To Easy Pizza Dough (here)
- 1 tablespoon Essential Garlic Oil (here), plus more for finishing
- ½ cup Anchoiade (here)
- 1 fennel bulb, thinly sliced on a mandoline
- 6 fresh ripe figs, such as black Mission, stemmed and quartered
- 1 tablespoon chopped fresh thyme
- Freshly ground black pepper

DIRECTIONS
1. Toss the onion slices with olive oil and salt and place in a cazuela. Roast slowly in the mouth of the oven, tossing frequently. Prevent the onions from burning by adding a splash of water

if needed. The onions will lose considerable volume, begin to color slightly, and become much sweeter. When the onions have deeply colored and lost most of their volume, after 20 minutes or so, remove the pan. Allow to cool.
2. Following the directions for a fully prepped oven, make sure your fire is at the desired cooking temperature with a roiling flame and a brushed and cleaned oven floor. You are now ready to make a pizza.
3. Stretch out the dough as shown in "How to Shape a Pizza" (here). Lightly dust your pizza peel with flour. Place your stretched dough directly on the peel and proceed to build the pizza.
4. Brush the stretched dough with the garlic oil and spread the anchoiade evenly over the dough, leaving a ½-inch border all the way around the outside. Distribute the caramelized onions and sliced fennel over the pie, followed by the quartered figs. Sprinkle the entire pie with a pinch of salt and the chopped thyme.
5. Slide the pizza into the oven and bake for 3 to 5 minutes, rotating once or twice to ensure even cooking. Remove the pizza to a cutting board and add a few grinds of black pepper. Slice into 6 or 8 wedges. Brush the crust edges with a quick pass of the garlic oil to finish.

ONION, ANCHOVY, AND NIÇOISE OLIVE PIZZA

MAKES ONE 10-INCH PIZZA
Prep time: 35 minutes
Cook time: 30 minutes

Ingredients

- ½ cup extra-virgin olive oil
- 4 cups sliced yellow onion
- Salt
- 2 tablespoons finely chopped fresh thyme
- 1 portion Elevated Pizza Dough (here)
- 2 tablespoons Essential Garlic Oil (here), plus more for finishing
- 10 salt-packed anchovies, rinsed, soaked, filleted (see Prep Tip), and halved lengthwise (40 pieces total)
- ½ cup pitted, halved niçoise olives
- Freshly ground black pepper

DIRECTIONS
1. Heat a wide-mouthed pan with a tight-fitting lid over high heat, add the olive oil and then the onions, and season with a generous teaspoon of salt. Stir to coat the onions in the oil and then cover the pot. Cook over high heat for 5 minutes, uncovering and stirring occasionally to prevent scorching.
2. After 5 minutes, or when the onions begin to soften in their own juice, uncover the pot and turn

the heat down to medium-low. Cook the onions for 20 minutes, stirring occasionally and adding a splash of water if they start to color. Stir in the chopped thyme, then spread the cooked onions in a single layer on a half sheet to facilitate cooling.

3. Following the directions for a fully prepped oven, make sure your fire is at the desired cooking temperature with a roiling flame and a brushed and cleaned oven floor. You are now ready to make a pizza.
4. Stretch out the dough as shown in "How to Shape a Pizza" (here). Lightly dust your pizza peel with flour. Place your stretched dough directly on the peel and proceed to build the pizza.
5. Brush the stretched dough with the garlic oil. Spread the cooled onions over the dough, leaving a ½-inch border. Arrange the sliced anchovy fillets in a diamond pattern and place an olive half in the "window" of each diamond.
6. Slide the pizza into the oven and bake for 3 to 5 minutes, rotating once or twice to ensure even cooking. Remove the pizza to a cutting board and add a few grinds of black pepper. Slice into 6 or 8 wedges. Brush the crust edges with a quick pass of the garlic oil to finish.

WHIPPED SALT COD AND POTATO PIZZA

MAKES ONE 10-INCH PIZZA

Prep time: 30 minutes for the salt cod, 15 minutes for the pizza

Cook time: 20 minutes for the salt cod, 5 minutes for the pizza

Ingredients

FOR THE WHIPPED SALT COD
- 1 pound salt cod
- 1 pound Yellow Finn or russet potatoes, peeled and quartered
- 2 cups water
- 2 cups whole milk
- ½ yellow onion, quartered
- 1 whole garlic clove, peeled
- 1 bay leaf
- 1 fresh thyme sprig
- ¾ cup extra-virgin olive oil
- 2 tablespoons garlic, pounded in a mortar and pestle
- Salt

FOR THE PIZZA
- 8 ounces Yellow Finn potatoes, sliced
- ⅛ inch thick
- Salt

- Extra-virgin olive oil
- 1 portion Basic Go-To Easy Pizza Dough (here)
- ½ cup Harissa (here)
- 1 egg
- Freshly ground black pepper

DIRECTIONS

TO MAKE THE WHIPPED SALT COD

1. The day before you plan to make this pizza, place the salt cod in a large bowl and cover with water. Soak in the refrigerator, replacing the water several times throughout the soaking process.
2. The next day, cook the potatoes in boiling salted water until easily pierced with the tip of a knife, about 10 minutes. Drain well, return to the warm pan, and allow to dry out until cool.
3. Drain the salt cod. In a large pot, combine the salt cod, water, milk, onion, whole garlic clove, bay leaf, and thyme. Cut a round of parchment paper large enough to fit over the pot and press it down on the fish. Make a slight tear in the paper to allow steam to escape.
4. Slowly bring the pot to a simmer over medium heat, then turn the heat down to a bare simmer and poach the fish until tender, 8 to 10 minutes. Lift the fish from the poaching liquid and cool slightly. Reserve ½ cup of the poaching liquid. Pick over the fish, removing any dark spots or bones. Transfer the fish to the bowl of an electric stand mixer fitted with the paddle attachment.
5. Warm the olive oil and pounded garlic over low heat until it begins to sizzle and immediately remove from the heat, being careful to not allow the garlic to color.
6. Gradually beat the cooked potatoes into the fish, moistening with a few drops of the reserved poaching liquid. Add the warm garlic oil and continue beating. Taste for seasoning—it may need salt, believe it or not. The mixture should be smooth and highly seasoned, and absorb the oil and poaching liquid. Set aside until ready to use (or cover and refrigerate if not using until the following day).

TO MAKE THE PIZZA

1. In a bowl, toss the sliced potatoes with a generous pinch of salt and moisten with a splash each of olive oil and water. Arrange the potatoes in a single layer on an unlined half sheet and roast in a very hot oven until they begin to take on color and soften, 4 to 7 minutes. Allow the potatoes to cool completely, taste, and adjust the seasoning with more salt if needed. Set aside until you're ready to build the pizza.
2. Following the directions for a fully prepped oven, make sure your fire is at the desired cooking temperature with a roiling flame and a brushed and cleaned oven floor. You are now ready to make a pizza.
3. Stretch out the dough as shown in "How to Shape a Pizza" (here). Lightly dust your pizza peel with flour. Place your stretched dough directly on the peel and proceed to build the pizza.
4. Brush the stretched dough evenly with the harissa, leaving a ½-inch border all the way around the outside. Next, layer the cooked potato slices, followed by small spoonfuls of the whipped

salt cod.

5. Carefully crack the egg into a small bowl. Discard the watery layer that surrounds the white, taking care to keep the yolk intact.
6. Slide the pizza into the oven and bake for 2 minutes to set the bottom of the crust. Remove the pie, carefully tip the egg onto the center of the pizza, and return it to the oven. Bake until the egg white is opaque but the yolk is still runny, another 2 to 3 minutes. Remove the pizza to a cutting board and add a few grinds of black pepper. Slice into 6 or 8 wedges.

FLATBREAD OF SMOKED SALMON AND CAVIAR

MAKES ONE 10-INCH PIZZA

Prep time: 15 minutes

Cook time: 3 to 5 minutes

Ingredients

- 1 portion North African Flatbread dough (here)
- ¼ cup thinly sliced red onion, soaked in ice water for 10 minutes
- ½ cup Wild Fennel Sauce (here)
- 4 ounces high-quality smoked salmon
- ¼ cup crème fraîche
- 1 ounce caviar or salmon roe (optional)
- 2 tablespoons finely chopped fresh chives
- Freshly ground black pepper

DIRECTIONS

1. Following the directions for a fully prepped oven, make sure your fire is at the desired cooking temperature with a roiling flame and a brushed and cleaned oven floor. You are now ready to make a pizza.
2. Stretch out the dough as shown in "How to Shape a Pizza" (here). Lightly dust your pizza peel with flour. Place your stretched dough directly on the peel and proceed to build the pizza.
3. Drain the onions from the ice water and dry thoroughly.
4. Brush the stretched dough with the fennel sauce, spreading evenly. Leave a ½-inch border around the outside of the dough. Slide the dough into the oven and bake for 3 to 5 minutes, rotating once or twice to ensure even cooking.
5. Remove the flatbread to a cutting board, and drape the smoked salmon slices over the pie. Garnish with the red onion. Drizzle over the crème fraîche, distribute the caviar or salmon roe evenly, if using, and garnish with the chopped chives. Slice into 6 or 8 wedges. Add a few grinds of black pepper.

ROASTED CLAM AND BACON PIZZA

MAKES ONE 10-INCH PIZZA

Prep time: 30 minutes

Cook time: 3 to 5 minutes

Ingredients

- 1 pound littleneck or cherrystone clams
- ¼ cup dry white wine
- Extra-virgin olive oil
- 1 portion Elevated Pizza Dough (here)
- 2 tablespoons Essential Garlic Oil (here), plus more for finishing
- ¼ cup Wild Fennel Sauce (here)
- ½ cup sliced fennel bulb, dressed with olive oil and salt
- 8 ounces smoked bacon, cooked until crispy and crumbled
- 2 tablespoons heavy cream
- Salt
- ¼ cup chopped fresh flat-leaf parsley
- 10 mint leaves, torn into bite-size pieces
- 1 lemon
- Freshly ground black pepper

DIRECTIONS

1. Following the directions for a fully prepped oven, make sure your fire is at the desired cooking temperature with a roiling flame and a brushed and cleaned oven floor.
2. Wash the clams thoroughly in a bowl of cold water, removing as much sandy grit as possible. Transfer the clams to a cazuela large enough for them to fit in a single layer, add the white wine, and drizzle with olive oil. Roast in the hottest part of the oven until the clams begin to open. Remove any clams as they open and return the cazuela to the oven to finish cooking the rest. Repeat until all the clams have opened. Discard any that remain closed. When cool enough to handle, strain the liquid from the cazuela into a small bowl and pull the clams from their shells, adding them to the roasting liquid as you go to keep them moist.
3. Stretch out the dough as shown in "How to Shape a Pizza" (here). Lightly dust your pizza peel with flour. Place your stretched dough directly on the peel and proceed to build the pizza.
4. Brush the stretched dough with the garlic oil and spread the fennel sauce evenly, leaving a ½-inch border all the way around the outside. Arrange the sliced fennel and the clams over the pie. Scatter the crumbled bacon on top. Drizzle with the cream. Sprinkle the entire pie with a pinch of salt.
5. Slide the pizza into the oven and bake for 3 to 5 minutes, rotating once or twice to ensure even cooking. Remove the pizza to a cutting board. In a small bowl, toss together the parsley and

mint. Dress with olive oil and salt and scatter over the pie. Give a big squeeze of lemon juice over the entire pizza and add a few grinds of black pepper. Slice into 6 or 8 wedges. Brush the crust edges with a quick pass of the garlic oil to finish.

SQUID PIZZA WITH CHERRY TOMATOES AND AIOLI

MAKES ONE 10-INCH PIZZA

Prep time: 30 minutes

Cook time: 3 to 5 minutes

Ingredients

- 1 portion Basic Go-To Easy Pizza Dough (here)
- 2 tablespoons Essential Garlic Oil (here), plus more for finishing
- ½ cup Wild Fennel Sauce (here)
- 1 cup arugula, packed tightly
- 1 cup halved cherry tomatoes, dressed with olive oil and salt
- 8 ounces fresh squid, cleaned and cut into rings and tentacles, dressed with olive oil and salt
- ¼ cup fresh basil leaves
- Salt
- 1 recipe Aïoli (here)

DIRECTIONS

1. Following the directions for a fully prepped oven, make sure your fire is at the desired cooking temperature with a roiling flame and a brushed and cleaned oven floor. You are now ready to make a pizza.
2. Stretch out the dough as shown in "How to Shape a Pizza" (here). Lightly dust your pizza peel with flour. Place your stretched dough directly on the peel and proceed to build the pizza.
3. Brush the stretched dough with the garlic oil and spread the fennel sauce evenly, leaving a ½-inch border all the way around the outside. Arrange the arugula, cherry tomatoes, and squid rings and tentacles. Garnish with the whole basil leaves, pressing lightly into the sauce. Season the entire pie with a pinch of salt.
4. Slide the pizza into the oven and bake for 3 to 5 minutes, rotating once or twice to ensure even cooking. Remove the pizza to a cutting board.
5. Thin the aïoli with a few drops of water or lemon juice to achieve a thick, pourable sauce. Drizzle liberally over the pie. Slice into 6 or 8 wedges. Brush the crust edges with a quick pass of the garlic oil to finish.

SHRIMP, SWEET PEPPER, AND CHERRY

TOMATO PIZZA WITH GREEN GARLIC

MAKES ONE 10-INCH PIZZA

Prep time: 30 minutes

Cook time: 3 to 5 minutes

Ingredients

- 1 cup Jimmy Nardello peppers, or a mix of sweet and hot peppers
- Extra-virgin olive oil
- Salt
- 1 portion Whole-Wheat Pizza Dough (here) or Spelt Pizza Dough (here)
- 1 tablespoon Essential Garlic Oil (here), plus more for finishing
- 2 tablespoons finely chopped green garlic (optional)
- ½ cup halved cherry tomatoes, seasoned with olive oil and salt
- 12 medium shrimp, peeled, deveined, and halved lengthwise
- ¼ cup fresh green or purple basil leaves
- 1 teaspoon Marash pepper flakes (optional)

DIRECTIONS

1. Remove the seeds and stems from the peppers, thinly slice, and dress them with olive oil and salt. Let them macerate for 10 minutes before you begin to make your pizza.
2. Following the directions for a fully prepped oven, make sure your fire is at the desired cooking temperature with a roiling flame and a brushed and cleaned oven floor. You are now ready to make a pizza.
3. Stretch out the dough as shown in "How to Shape a Pizza" (here). Lightly dust your pizza peel with flour. Place your stretched dough directly on the peel and proceed to build the pizza.
4. Brush the stretched dough with the garlic oil and scatter the peppers and green garlic (if using) evenly, leaving a ½-inch border all the way around the outside. Arrange the cherry tomatoes, shrimp, and basil over the pie. Sprinkle the entire pie with a pinch of salt. Garnish with the Marash pepper flakes, if using.
5. Slide the pizza into the oven and bake for 3 to 5 minutes, rotating once or twice to ensure even cooking. Remove the pizza to a cutting board and slice into 6 or 8 wedges. Brush the crust edges with a quick pass of the garlic oil to finish.

PIZZA MARGHERITA

MAKES ONE 10-INCH PIZZA

Prep time: 10 minutes

Cook time: 3 to 5 minutes

Ingredients

- 1 portion Basic Go-To Easy Pizza Dough (here)
- 1 tablespoon Essential Garlic Oil (here), plus more for finishing
- ½ cup Simple Tomato Sauce (here)
- ½ cup shredded part-skim mozzarella or 4 ounces buffalo mozzarella, thinly sliced
- 8 fresh basil leaves
- Salt
- Parmesan cheese
- Freshly ground black pepper

DIRECTIONS

1. Following the directions for a fully prepped oven, make sure your fire is at the desired cooking temperature with a roiling flame and a brushed and cleaned oven floor. You are now ready to make a pizza.
2. Stretch out the dough as shown in "How to Shape a Pizza" (here). Lightly dust your pizza peel with flour. Place your stretched dough directly on the peel and proceed to build the pizza.
3. Brush the stretched dough with the garlic oil and spread the tomato sauce evenly over the dough, leaving a ½-inch border all the way around the outside. Arrange the shredded or sliced cheese, whichever you prefer, distributing evenly. Garnish the dressed pie with the basil leaves, pressing lightly into the sauce and cheese. Season the entire pie with a pinch of salt.
4. Slide the pizza into the oven and bake for 3 to 5 minutes, rotating once or twice to ensure even cooking. Remove the pizza to a cutting board, grate Parmesan cheese over the entire pie, and add a few grinds of black pepper. Slice into 6 or 8 wedges. Brush the crust edges with a quick pass of the garlic oil to finish.

GLUTEN-FREE PESTO PIZZA

MAKES ONE 9-BY-13-INCH PIZZA

Prep time: 30 minutes

Cook time: about 10 minutes

Ingredients

- 1 cup fresh sweet corn kernels
- Extra-virgin olive oil
- Salt
- 1 portion Gluten-Free Pizza Dough (here), prebaked
- 4 tablespoons Essential Garlic Oil (here), divided, plus more for finishing
- ¾ cup Basic Pesto (here)
- 1 cup thinly sliced yellow summer squash
- 1 cup halved cherry tomatoes

- 2 ounces goat cheese, crumbled
- Freshly ground black pepper
- Parmesan cheese

DIRECTIONS

1. Toss the fresh corn kernels with olive oil and salt and transfer to a cazuela large enough to hold the corn in a single shallow layer. Roast in the wood oven for 4 to 6 minutes, tossing once to prevent scorching. Remove from the oven and allow to cool before building the pizza.
2. Following the directions for a fully prepped oven, make sure your fire is at the desired cooking temperature with a roiling flame and a brushed and cleaned oven floor. You are now ready to make a pizza.
3. Prebake the gluten-free dough, as described in the recipe (here). Remove the cooled dough from the quarter sheet pan and build the pizza directly on the wooden peel.
4. Brush the stretched dough with 2 tablespoons of the garlic oil and spread the pesto evenly over the dough, leaving a ½-inch border all the way around the outside. In a separate bowl, toss the squash slices with a splash of olive oil and season with a generous pinch of salt. Arrange the slices in a thin layer over the sauce. Mix the roasted corn and the cherry tomatoes together, adjust the seasoning, and scatter over the pizza. Dot the pie with the goat cheese and drizzle the entire pizza with the remaining 2 tablespoons garlic oil.
5. Slide the pizza into the oven long enough to warm the pizza toppings through and finish cooking the gluten-free dough, about 3 minutes.
6. Remove from the oven and add a few grinds of black pepper. Grate the Parmesan cheese over the pie. Slice into 10 rectangles. Brush the crust edges with a quick pass of the garlic oil to finish.

PIZZA WITH FRESH TOMATOES, GYPSY PEPPERS, AND CAPERS

MAKES ONE 10-INCH PIZZA

Prep time: 30 minutes

Cook time: 3 to 5 minutes

Ingredients

- 1 tablespoon salt-packed capers, rinsed
- 1 portion Basic Go-To Easy Pizza Dough (here)
- 2 tablespoons Essential Garlic Oil (here), plus more for dressing and finishing
- ¼ cup Oven-Roasted Red Sauce (here)
- 8 ounces ripe organic heirloom tomatoes, very thinly sliced and drained
- Salt
- ½ cup shredded part-skim mozzarella

- ½ cup seeded and very thinly sliced gypsy peppers
- 2 tablespoons roughly chopped fresh marjoram or oregano

1. Put the capers in a small bowl and cover with water. Set aside and allow to soak for 10 minutes. Lift the capers from the water and drain on a paper towel, then roughly chop and set aside until ready to use.
2. Following the directions for a fully prepped oven, make sure your fire is at the desired cooking temperature with a roiling flame and a brushed and cleaned oven floor. You are now ready to make a pizza.
3. Stretch out the dough as shown in "How to Shape a Pizza" (here). Lightly dust your pizza peel with flour. Place your stretched dough directly on the peel and proceed to build the pizza.
4. Brush the dough with the garlic oil and spoon over the red sauce in a few random streaks. Arrange the drained tomatoes, taking care not to overlap the slices. Season the tomato slices with a good pinch or two of salt. Then evenly top with the shredded cheese.
5. In a small bowl, toss the sliced peppers with a good pinch of salt and a splash of garlic oil. Scatter the dressed peppers over the pie.
6. Slide the pizza into the oven and bake for 3 to 5 minutes, rotating once or twice to ensure even cooking. Remove the pizza to a cutting board and slice into 6 or 8 wedges. Garnish with the chopped capers and marjoram. Brush the crust edges with a quick pass of the garlic oil to finish.

ASPARAGUS AND FAVA BEAN PIZZA WITH TAPENADE

MAKES ONE 10-INCH PIZZA

Prep time: 30 minutes

Cook time: 3 to 5 minutes

Ingredients

- 3 thick asparagus spears
- Extra-virgin olive oil
- Salt
- 1 portion Whole-Wheat Pizza Dough (here) or Spelt Pizza Dough (here)
- 2 tablespoons Essential Garlic Oil (here), plus more for finishing
- ½ cup Tapenade (here)
- 1 cup fava beans, shelled and blanched (see Prep Tip)
- 2 ounces fresh ricotta cheese
- Parmesan cheese
- Freshly ground black pepper
- 2 tablespoons fresh mint leaves, torn into bite-size pieces

DIRECTIONS

1. Prepare the asparagus by snapping off the woody stems and discarding. Using a mandoline, carefully slice the raw asparagus lengthwise, creating paper-thin ribbons. Toss the asparagus ribbons in a small bowl with a splash of olive oil and a pinch of salt.
2. Following the directions for a fully prepped oven, make sure your fire is at the desired cooking temperature with a roiling flame and a brushed and cleaned oven floor. You are now ready to make a pizza.
3. Stretch out the dough as shown in "How to Shape a Pizza" (here). Lightly dust your pizza peel with flour. Place your stretched dough directly on the peel and proceed to build the pizza.
4. Brush the stretched dough with the garlic oil and spread the tapenade evenly over the dough, leaving a ½-inch border all the way around the outside. Arrange the dressed asparagus ribbons over the dough, followed by the prepared fava beans. Dollop small spoonfuls of the ricotta around the pie. Season the pie with a pinch of salt.
5. Slide the pizza into the oven and bake for 3 to 5 minutes, rotating once or twice to ensure even cooking. Remove the pizza to a cutting board, grate the Parmesan cheese over the entire pie, and add a few grinds of black pepper. Sprinkle the entire pizza with the chopped mint. Slice into 6 or 8 wedges. Brush the crust edges with a quick pass of the garlic oil to finish.

EGGPLANT PIZZA WITH FRESH MOZZARELLA AND OVEN-DRIED HERBS

MAKES ONE 10-INCH PIZZA

Prep time: 40 minutes

Cook time: 3 to 5 minutes

Ingredients

- 1 medium globe eggplant
- 1 teaspoon salt
- ¼ cup plus 1 tablespoon extra-virgin olive oil, divided
- 2 teaspoons mixed oven-dried herbs, such as oregano or marjoram (see Prep Tip)
- 1 portion Elevated Pizza Dough (here)
- 2 tablespoons Essential Garlic Oil (here), plus more for finishing
- ½ cup Oven-Roasted Red Sauce (here)
- 4 ounces buffalo mozzarella, thinly sliced
- Salt
- Freshly ground black pepper

- Parmesan cheese

DIRECTIONS

1. Use a vegetable peeler to peel some of the skin from the eggplant in a striped pattern. The skin can cook up tough, but a little toughness is fine. Slice into ⅛-inch-thick rounds and season with the salt, ¼ cup of olive oil, and the oven-dried herbs. Toss well to combine. Oil a half sheet pan with the remaining 1 tablespoon of olive oil and arrange the eggplant in a single layer. Roast in the window of the wood oven for 4 to 5 minutes to soften the eggplant; rotate as needed to avoid burning the slices. Allow to cool before building the pizza.
2. Following the directions for a fully prepped oven, make sure your fire is at the desired cooking temperature with a roiling flame and a brushed and cleaned oven floor. You are now ready to make a pizza.
3. Stretch out the dough as shown in "How to Shape a Pizza" (here). Lightly dust your pizza peel with flour. Place your stretched dough directly on the peel and proceed to build the pizza.
4. Brush the stretched dough with the garlic oil and spread the red sauce evenly over the dough, leaving a ½-inch border all the way around the outside. Arrange the eggplant slices in a thin layer over the sauce. Layer on the mozzarella. Season the entire pie with a pinch of salt.
5. Slide the pizza into the oven and bake for 3 to 5 minutes, rotating once or twice to ensure even cooking. Remove the pizza to a cutting board and add a few grinds of black pepper. Grate the Parmesan cheese over the entire pizza. Slice into 6 or 8 wedges. Brush the crust edges with a quick pass of the garlic oil to finish.

WHOLE-WHEAT PIZZA WITH GREENS, RAPINI, PINE NUTS, AND RICOTTA SALATA

MAKES ONE 10-INCH PIZZA

Prep time: 40 minutes

Cook time: about 10 minutes

Ingredients

- 8 ounces Swiss chard, Lacinato kale, or spinach
- ¼ cup chopped rapini
- 1 tablespoon extra-virgin olive oil
- Salt
- 1 portion Whole-Wheat Pizza Dough (here)
- 1 tablespoon Essential Garlic Oil (here), plus more for finishing
- ½ cup Salsa Bianca (here)
- 2 ounces ricotta salata, grated

- 4 fresh nasturtium flowers, petals only (optional)
- Freshly ground black pepper

DIRECTIONS

1. First, precook the two main vegetables that top this pizza. Blanch the greens in salted boiling water, drain thoroughly, squeeze out any excess moisture, and chop. Sauté the chopped rapini in a covered pan in 1 tablespoon of olive oil, a splash of water, and a pinch of salt. Cook for 3 to 5 minutes. Allow to cool before building the pizza.
2. Following the directions for a fully prepped oven, make sure your fire is at the desired cooking temperature with a roiling flame and a brushed and cleaned oven floor. You are now ready to make a pizza.
3. Stretch out the dough as shown in "How to Shape a Pizza" (here). Lightly dust your pizza peel with flour. Place your stretched dough directly on the peel and proceed to build the pizza.
4. Brush the stretched dough with the garlic oil and spread the salsa bianca evenly over the dough, leaving a ½-inch border all the way around the outside. Arrange the greens and rapini in a thin layer over the sauce. Take care not to overcrowd the pizza. Season the entire pie with a pinch of salt.
5. Slide the pizza into the oven and bake for 3 to 5 minutes, rotating once or twice to ensure even cooking. Remove the pizza to a cutting board. Garnish with grated ricotta salata, and scatter the flower petals about, if using. Add a few grinds of black pepper. Slice into 6 or 8 wedges. Brush the crust edges with a quick pass of the garlic oil to finish.

SQUASH AND SQUASH BLOSSOM PIZZA WITH CHERRY TOMATOES

MAKES ONE 10-INCH PIZZA

Prep time: 20 minutes

Cook time: 3 to 5 minutes

Ingredients

- 1 portion Basic Go-To Easy Pizza Dough (here)
- 1 tablespoon Essential Garlic Oil (here), plus more for finishing
- ½ cup Salsa Bianca (here)
- ½ cup thinly sliced yellow summer squash
- 3 fresh squash blossoms, stems and pistils removed, torn into 3-inch-wide ribbons
- ½ cup halved cherry tomatoes
- Salt
- Parmesan cheese
- Freshly ground black pepper

DIRECTIONS

1. Following the directions for a fully prepped oven, make sure your fire is at the desired cooking temperature with a roiling flame and a brushed and cleaned oven floor. You are now ready to make a pizza.
2. Stretch out the dough as shown in "How to Shape a Pizza" (here). Lightly dust your pizza peel with flour. Place your stretched dough directly on the peel and proceed to build the pizza.
3. Brush the stretched dough with the garlic oil and spread the salsa bianca evenly over the dough, leaving a ½-inch border all the way around the outside. Arrange the slices of yellow squash so they don't overlap one another, fill in the spaces with the torn squash blossoms, and, finally, scatter the halved cherry tomatoes. Sprinkle the entire pie with a pinch of salt.
4. Slide the pizza into the oven and bake for 3 to 5 minutes, rotating once or twice to ensure even cooking. Remove the pizza to a cutting board, grate Parmesan cheese over the entire pie, and add a few grinds of black pepper. Slice into 6 or 8 wedges. Brush the crust edges with a quick pass of the garlic oil to finish.

ARTICHOKES, LEEKS, AND GREMOLATA PIZZA

MAKES ONE 10-INCH PIZZA

Prep time: 30 minutes

Cook time: about 10 minutes

Ingredients

- 1 large leek
- 1 tablespoon olive oil, plus more for dressing
- Salt
- 1 portion Whole-Wheat Pizza Dough (here) or Spelt Pizza Dough (here)
- 1 tablespoon Essential Garlic Oil (here), plus more for finishing
- ¼ cup Simple Tomato Sauce (here)
- 2 ounces fresh ricotta
- ½ cup baby artichokes, outer leaves removed
- 2 tablespoons gremolata (see A Closer Look)

DIRECTIONS

1. Begin by peeling away the outer layer of the leek. Trim and discard the root end and the tough upper green portion. Cut in half lengthwise, then crosswise into ¼-inch-thick slices. Rinse in a bowl of water if there is any grit in between the layers. Drain and toss the leek in 1 tablespoon of olive oil, then season with salt. Transfer to a cazuela large enough to hold the leeks in a single layer. Cook, stirring often, in a medium-hot section of the oven. Be careful to not let them burn, as they will become tough. Add a splash of water if the cazuela begins

to dry out before the leeks are cooked through and soft, about 5 to 7 minutes. Remove from the oven and allow to cool before building the pizza.
2. Following the directions for a fully prepped oven, make sure your fire is at the desired cooking temperature with a roiling flame and a brushed and cleaned oven floor. You are now ready to make a pizza.
3. Stretch out the dough as shown in "How to Shape a Pizza" (here). Lightly dust your pizza peel with flour. Place your stretched dough directly on the peel and proceed to build the pizza.
4. Brush the stretched dough with the garlic oil and spread the tomato sauce lightly in streaks. Arrange the stewed leeks evenly over the sauce, and add small spoonfuls of the ricotta around the pie. Season the pie with a pinch of salt. Quickly slice the artichokes as thinly as possible on a mandoline and place in a small bowl. Season with a few drops of olive oil and salt to inhibit burning while in the oven. Scatter evenly over the pizza.
5. Slide the pizza into the oven and bake for 3 to 5 minutes, rotating once or twice to ensure even cooking. Remove the pizza to a cutting board and slice into 6 or 8 wedges. Garnish generously with the gremolata. Brush the crust edges with a quick pass of the garlic oil to finish.

ARTICHOKE PIZZA WITH ROASTED RED ONIONS AND FRESH THYME

MAKES ONE 10-INCH PIZZA

Prep time: 20 minutes

Cook time: about 15 minutes

Ingredients

- 1 medium sweet red onion, cut crosswise into ½-inch-thick slices
- Salt
- 2 tablespoons Essential Garlic Oil (here), divided, plus more for finishing
- 1 portion Basic Go-To Easy Pizza Dough (here)
- ¼ cup Salsa Bianca (here)
- ½ cup shredded part-skim mozzarella
- ½ cup baby artichokes, outer leaves removed
- Extra-virgin olive oil
- 1 tablespoon chopped fresh thyme

DIRECTIONS

1. Season the onion slices with salt and brush both sides with 1 tablespoon of garlic oil, trying to keep the rings intact. Arrange in a single layer on a half sheet and roast slowly in the window of the oven until the onion slices soften, caramelize, and char slightly, about 10 minutes. Rotate the sheet pan often for even cooking and turn the slices over if they begin to color too

strongly on the bottom. Allow to cool before building the pizza.
2. Following the directions for a fully prepped oven, make sure your fire is at the desired cooking temperature with a roiling flame and a brushed and cleaned oven floor. You are now ready to make a pizza.
3. Stretch out the dough as shown in "How to Shape a Pizza" (here). Lightly dust your pizza peel with flour. Place your stretched dough directly on the peel and proceed to build the pizza.
4. Brush the stretched dough with the remaining 1 tablespoon of garlic oil and spread the salsa bianca evenly over the dough, leaving a ½-inch border all the way around the outside. Arrange the shredded cheese evenly over the sauce, and top with the roasted red onions. Season the pie with a pinch of salt.
5. Quickly slice the artichokes as thinly as possible on a mandoline and place in a small bowl. Season with a few drops of olive oil and salt to inhibit burning while in the oven. Scatter evenly over the pizza.
6. Slide the pizza into the oven and bake for 3 to 5 minutes, rotating once or twice to ensure even cooking. Remove the pizza to a cutting board and slice into 6 or 8 wedges. Garnish with the thyme. Brush the crust edges with a quick pass of the garlic oil to finish.

ROASTED BUTTERNUT SQUASH, ROQUEFORT, AND WALNUT PIZZA

MAKES ONE 10-INCH PIZZA

Prep time: 30 minutes

Cook time: about 10 minutes

Ingredients

- ½ butternut squash, peeled, seeded, and cut into ⅛-inch-thick slices
- 2 tablespoons Essential Garlic Oil ,divided, plus more for finishing
- Salt
- 1 portion Elevated Pizza Dough
- ¼ cup shredded part-skim mozzarella
- 2 ounces Roquefort or domestic blue cheese, crumbled
- Parmesan cheese
- Freshly ground black pepper
- ¼ cup walnuts, toasted, skinned, and roughly chopped
- 1 bunch fresh sage, leaves picked and fried (see Prep Tip)

DIRECTIONS
1. Toss the squash slices in 1 tablespoon of garlic oil and season with salt. Arrange on a half sheet pan in a single layer and roast in a medium-hot oven for 4 to 5 minutes or until lightly browned and tender. Allow the squash to cool before building the pie.

2. Following the directions for a fully prepped oven, make sure your fire is at the desired cooking temperature with a roiling flame and a brushed and cleaned oven floor. You are now ready to make a pizza.
3. Stretch out the dough as shown in "How to Shape a Pizza" (here). Lightly dust your pizza peel with flour. Place your stretched dough directly on the peel and proceed to build the pizza.
4. Brush the stretched dough with the remaining 1 tablespoon of garlic oil and spread the shredded mozzarella evenly over the dough, leaving a ½-inch border all the way around the outside. Arrange the roasted squash slices so they don't overlap, and fill in the spaces with the crumbled Roquefort. Sprinkle the entire pie with a pinch of salt.
5. Slide the pizza into the oven and bake for 3 to 5 minutes, rotating once or twice to ensure even cooking. Remove the pizza to a cutting board, grate Parmesan cheese over the entire pie, and add a few grinds of black pepper. Crumble the walnuts over the pizza and arrange the whole fried sage leaves. Slice into 6 or 8 wedges. Brush the crust edges with a quick pass of the garlic oil to finish.

A GREEN PIE
ZUCCHINI, RAPINI, AND PESTO

MAKES ONE 10-INCH PIZZA

Prep time: 20 minutes

Cook time: about 10 minutes

Ingredients

- 3 or 4 zucchini, thinly sliced on a mandoline
- 2 tablespoons Essential Garlic Oil (here), divided, plus more for finishing
- Salt
- 1 bunch rapini
- 1 tablespoon extra-virgin olive oil
- 1 portion Whole-Wheat Pizza Dough (here) or Spelt Pizza Dough (here)
- 4 ounces fresh buffalo mozzarella, sliced into rounds
- ¼ cup Basic Pesto (here)
- Parmesan cheese
- 1 teaspoon dried chili flakes

DIRECTIONS
1. Toss the sliced zucchini in 1 tablespoon of garlic oil and season with salt. Chop the rapini and sauté in a covered pan in 1 tablespoon of olive oil, a splash of water, and a pinch of salt. Cook for 3 to 5 minutes. Allow to cool before building the pizza.

2. Following the directions for a fully prepped oven, make sure your fire is at the desired cooking temperature with a roiling flame and a brushed and cleaned oven floor.
3. Stretch out the dough as shown in "How to Shape a Pizza" (here). Lightly dust your pizza peel with flour. Place your stretched dough directly on the peel and proceed to build the pizza.
4. Brush the stretched dough with the remaining 1 tablespoon garlic oil and arrange the zucchini evenly over the dough, leaving a ½-inch border all the way around the outside. Spoon over the cooked rapini and top with the mozzarella. Drizzle the pesto over the pizza.
5. Slide the pizza into the oven and bake for 3 to 5 minutes, rotating once or twice to ensure even cooking. Remove the pizza to a cutting board, grate Parmesan cheese over the entire pie, and sprinkle on the chili flakes. Slice into 6 or 8 wedges. Brush the crust edges with a quick pass of the garlic oil to finish.

FRESH PORCINI MUSHROOM PIZZA

MAKES ONE 10-INCH PIZZA

Prep time: 30 minutes

Cook time: 15 minutes

Ingredients

- 1 pound fresh porcini mushrooms
- 3 tablespoons Essential Garlic Oil ,divided, plus more for finishing
- Salt
- 1 portion Spelt Pizza Dough ,Elevated Pizza Dough ,or Basic Go-To Easy Pizza Dough
- 4 ounces imported Fontina Val d'Aosta cheese, grated
- Parmesan cheese
- Freshly ground black pepper
- 2 tablespoons torn fresh mint leaves

DIRECTIONS

1. Wipe the porcini free of any dirt that might still be attached with a damp towel and cut into ⅛-inch-thick slices. Toss the sliced mushrooms in 1 tablespoon of garlic oil and spread out in a single layer on a half sheet, then season with salt. Roast slowly in the window of the wood oven, 7 to 10 minutes. Allow to cool before building the pizza.
2. Following the directions for a fully prepped oven, make sure your fire is at the desired cooking temperature with a roiling flame and a brushed and cleaned oven floor. You are now ready to make a pizza.
3. Stretch out the dough as shown in "How to Shape a Pizza" (here). Lightly dust your pizza peel with flour. Place your stretched dough directly on the peel and proceed to build the pizza.
4. Brush the stretched dough with the remaining 2 tablespoons garlic oil and distribute the shredded Fontina evenly over the dough, leaving a ½-inch border all the way around the outside. Distribute the roasted mushrooms evenly. Season with a pinch of salt.

5. Slide the pizza into the oven and bake for 3 to 5 minutes, rotating once or twice to ensure even cooking. Remove the pizza to a cutting board, grate Parmesan cheese over the entire pie, and add a few grinds of black pepper. Scatter the torn mint over all. Slice into 6 or 8 wedges. Brush the crust edges with a quick pass of the garlic oil to finish.

MOREL MUSHROOM PIZZA WITH CREAM AND A SUNNY-SIDE UP EGG

MAKES ONE 10-INCH PIZZA

Prep time: 40 minutes

Cook time: about 25 minutes

Ingredients

- 1 cup morel mushrooms, sliced, washed, and drained (see A Closer Look)
- Salt
- 2 tablespoons unsalted butter
- 1 teaspoon chopped fresh thyme
- 3 thick asparagus spears
- Extra-virgin olive oil
- 1 extra-large egg
- 1 portion Elevated Pizza Dough (here)
- 2 tablespoons Essential Garlic Oil (here), plus more for finishing
- ¼ cup shredded part-skim mozzarella
- 2 tablespoons heavy cream
- Parmesan cheese
- Freshly ground black pepper

DIRECTIONS

1. Preheat a cast iron skillet large enough to hold the sliced morels in a single layer by placing it in a high-heat section of the oven for 5 minutes. Season the morels with a generous pinch of salt and add to the preheated skillet. Cook until all the liquid in the pan has evaporated and the mushrooms begin to sizzle rather than steam, 8 to 10 minutes. Stir in the butter and thyme and return the skillet to the oven for another 3 minutes. Remove and allow to cool until ready to build the pizza.
2. Prepare the asparagus by snapping off the woody stems and discarding. Using a mandoline, carefully slice the raw asparagus lengthwise, creating paper-thin ribbons. Toss the asparagus ribbons in a small bowl with a splash of olive oil and a pinch of salt.
3. Carefully crack the egg into a small bowl. Discard the watery layer that surrounds the white, taking care to keep the yolk intact.
4. Following the directions for a fully prepped oven, make sure your fire is at the desired cooking

temperature with a roiling flame and a brushed and cleaned oven floor. You are now ready to make a pizza.

5. Stretch out the dough as shown in "How to Shape a Pizza" (here). Lightly dust your pizza peel with flour. Place your stretched dough directly on the peel and proceed to build the pizza.
6. Brush the stretched dough with the garlic oil and spread the shredded cheese evenly over the dough, leaving a ½-inch border all the way around the outside. Arrange the dressed asparagus ribbons over the dough, followed by the cooked morels. Drizzle the assembled pizza with the heavy cream and season the entire pie with a pinch of salt.
7. Slide the pizza into the oven and bake for 2 minutes to set the bottom of the crust. Remove the pie, carefully tip the cracked egg into the center of the pizza, and return it to the oven. Bake until the egg white is opaque but the yolk is still runny, another 2 to 3 minutes.
8. Remove the pizza to a cutting board, grate Parmesan cheese over the entire pie, and add a few grinds of black pepper. Slice into 6 or 8 wedges, being careful to cut around the unbroken yolk. Brush the crust edges with a quick pass of the garlic oil to finish. Enjoy the pizza by dunking a slice into the softly cooked egg yolk.

STINGING NETTLE AND CHANTERELLE MUSHROOM PIZZA

MAKES ONE 10-INCH PIZZA

Prep time: 35 minutes

Cook time: about 20 minutes

Ingredients

- 2 cups stinging nettles, woody stems removed
- 8 ounces chanterelle mushrooms
- Salt
- 3 tablespoons Essential Garlic Oil (here), divided, plus more for finishing
- 1 portion Basic Go-To Easy Pizza Dough (here)
- ½ cup Simple Tomato Sauce (here)
- ½ cup shredded part-skim mozzarella
- 1 tablespoon extra-virgin olive oil
- Aged pecorino romano
- Freshly ground black pepper

DIRECTIONS

1. Fill a bowl with water large enough to hold the nettles, and soak them for 5 minutes. Agitate the nettles once or twice to loosen any dirt. Using tongs, lift them from the water, leaving the dirt behind, and drain thoroughly in a colander. Set aside until ready to use.
2. Wipe away any dirt that may still be attached to the chanterelle mushrooms. Slice them into

small chunks of roughly the same size and follow the directions for cleaning mushrooms outlined for morels here.

3. Following the directions for a fully prepped oven, make sure your fire is at the desired cooking temperature with a roiling flame and a brushed and cleaned oven floor.
4. Preheat a cast iron skillet, large enough to hold the sliced chanterelles in a single layer, by placing it in a high-heat section of the oven for 5 minutes. Season the chanterelles with a generous pinch of salt and add to the preheated skillet. Cook until all the liquid in the pan has evaporated and the mushrooms begin to sizzle rather than steam, 8 to 10 minutes. Remove the pan and add 1 tablespoon of garlic oil to the mushrooms, stirring to evenly coat, and cook for another 2 to 3 minutes. Remove from the oven and allow to cool until ready to build the pizza.
5. Stretch out the dough as shown in "How to Shape a Pizza" (here). Lightly dust your pizza peel with flour. Place your stretched dough directly on the peel and proceed to build the pizza.
6. Brush the stretched dough with the remaining 2 tablespoons garlic oil and spread the tomato sauce evenly over the dough, leaving a ½-inch border all the way around the outside. Arrange the shredded cheese, distributing evenly. Spread the cooked chanterelles over the cheese. In a small bowl, dress the nettles with 1 tablespoon of olive oil and a generous pinch of salt. Toss using kitchen tongs to avoid being stung. Pile the nettles on the pizza in a liberal heap.
7. Slide the pizza into the oven and bake for 3 to 5 minutes, rotating once or twice to ensure even cooking. Remove the pizza to a cutting board, shave the aged pecorino romano cheese over the entire pie, and add a few grinds of black pepper. Slice into 6 or 8 wedges. Brush the crust edges with a quick pass of the garlic oil to finish.

BLACK TRUFFLE AND FONTINA PIZZA

MAKES ONE 10-INCH PIZZA

Prep time: 25 minutes

Cook time: 3 to 5 minutes

Ingredients

- 8 ounces Yellow Finn potatoes, cut into ⅛-inch-thick slices
- Salt
- Extra-virgin olive oil
- 1 portion Elevated Pizza Dough (here)
- 2 tablespoons Essential Garlic Oil (here), plus more for finishing
- 1 fresh black truffle
- 4 ounces Fontina Val d'Aosta cheese, shredded
- Parmesan cheese
- Freshly ground black pepper

DIRECTIONS

1. In a bowl, toss the potato slices with a generous pinch of salt and moisten with a splash each of olive oil and water. Arrange the potatoes in a single layer on a half sheet and roast in a very hot oven until they begin to take on color and soften, 4 to 7 minutes. Allow the potatoes to cool completely, taste, and adjust the seasoning with more salt if needed. Set aside until you're ready to build the pizza.
2. Following the directions for a fully prepped oven, make sure your fire is at the desired cooking temperature with a roiling flame and a brushed and cleaned oven floor. You are now ready to make a pizza.
3. Stretch out the dough as shown in "How to Shape a Pizza" (here). Lightly dust your pizza peel with flour. Place your stretched dough directly on the peel and proceed to build the pizza.
4. Brush the dough with the garlic oil and sprinkle a pinch of salt over the entire pie. Using a truffle slicer or a mandoline or a very sharp knife, slice the truffle as thinly as possible and cover the entire pie with the slices. Top the truffles with the Fontina, and add a few gratings of Parmesan over all.
5. Slide the pizza into the oven and bake for 3 to 5 minutes, rotating once or twice to ensure even cooking. Remove the pizza to a cutting board and add a few grinds of black pepper. Slice into 6 or 8 wedges. Brush the crust edges with a quick pass of the garlic oil to finish.

THREE-CHEESE CALZONE

MAKES ONE 8-INCH HALF-MOON CALZONE

Prep time: 5 minutes

Cook time: 7 to 10 minutes

Ingredients

- 1 portion Basic Go-To Easy Pizza Dough (here)
- ¼ cup Simple Tomato Sauce (here)
- ¼ cup shredded part-skim mozzarella cheese
- 2 ounces imported provolone, grated
- 1 ounce goat cheese, crumbled
- 1 tablespoon extra-virgin olive oil, plus more for finishing
- 1 tablespoon chopped fresh flat-leaf parsley
- Salt
- Freshly ground black pepper

DIRECTIONS

1. Following the directions for a fully prepped oven, make sure your fire is at the desired cooking temperature with a roiling flame and a brushed and cleaned oven floor. You are now ready to make a calzone.
2. Begin by dusting your work surface with a small amount of flour. Stretch the pizza dough by

hand to a thin disc as described in "How to Shape a Pizza" (here). Dust the dough with a small amount of flour, turn over, and dust the other side. Using a rolling pin, gently roll the dough into a large, even, very thin circle. Continue to roll the dough, adding more flour as needed to prevent sticking. Transfer the dough to a lightly floured pizza peel.

3. Build the calzone on the half of the dough closest to you, as it will be folded over to create a half-moon shape. Spread the tomato sauce over the dough. Be sure to leave a 1-inch border to allow for a proper seal. Arrange the mozzarella, then the provolone, and finally the goat cheese over all. Drizzle the olive oil over the cheeses and sprinkle on the parsley. Season with salt and pepper.
4. In one quick motion, grasp the upper, undressed portion of dough and fold it over to meet the opposite edge, creating a half moon. Starting at one edge, seal the dough by pinching and rolling it over onto itself. Continue until the calzone is sealed. Tear a 1-inch hole in the top of the dough to release steam when baking.
5. Slide the calzone directly onto the oven floor and bake, rotating once or twice, until it is nicely puffed and browned, 7 to 10 minutes. Remove from the oven and brush the entire calzone with a small amount of olive oil to give it a glossy shine.

THREE-MEAT CALZONE

MAKES ONE 8-INCH HALF-MOON CALZONE

Prep time: 15 minutes

Cook time: 7 to 10 minutes

Ingredients

- 1 portion Basic Go-To Easy Pizza Dough (here)
- ¼ cup Simple Tomato Sauce (here)
- ¼ cup shredded part-skim mozzarella cheese
- 2 ounces pork sausage, crumbled and precooked (see Prep Tip)
- 2 ounces Genoa-style salami, cut into thin matchsticks
- 1 tablespoon chopped fresh flat-leaf parsley
- 1 teaspoon chopped fresh sage
- Freshly ground black pepper
- 2 slices prosciutto
- Extra-virgin olive oil

DIRECTIONS

1. Following the directions for a fully prepped oven, make sure your fire is at the desired cooking temperature with a roiling flame and a brushed and cleaned oven floor. You are now ready to make a calzone.
2. Begin by dusting your work surface with a small amount of flour. Stretch the pizza dough by hand to a thin disc as described in "How to Shape a Pizza" (here). Dust the dough with a

small amount of flour, turn over, and dust the other side. Using a rolling pin, gently roll the dough into a large, even, very thin circle. Continue to roll the dough, adding more flour as needed to prevent sticking. Transfer the dough to a lightly floured pizza peel.

3. Build the calzone on the half of the dough closest to you, as it will be folded over to create a half-moon shape. Spread the tomato sauce over the dough. Be sure to leave a 1-inch border to allow for a proper seal. Layer the shredded cheese, followed by the sausage and salami. Toss the parsley and sage together and sprinkle over the fillings. Season with freshly ground pepper. Lay the prosciutto slices over the entire half-moon in one single layer.

4. In one quick motion, grasp the upper, undressed portion of dough and fold it over to meet the opposite edge, creating a half moon. Starting at one edge, seal the dough by pinching and rolling it over onto itself. Continue until the calzone is sealed. Tear a 1-inch hole in the top of the dough to release steam when baking.

5. Slide the calzone directly onto the oven floor and bake, rotating once or twice, until it is nicely puffed and browned, 7 to 10 minutes. Remove from the oven and brush the entire calzone with a small amount of olive oil to give it a glossy shine.

THREE-VEGETABLE CALZONE

MAKES ONE 8-INCH HALF-MOON CALZONE

Prep time: 40 minutes

Cook time: about 30 minutes

Ingredients

- 3 thick asparagus spears
- Extra-virgin olive oil
- 1 teaspoon salt, plus more for seasoning
- 1 head radicchio
- 1 tablespoon red wine vinegar
- ½ cup baby artichokes, prepared (see Prep Tip)
- 1 portion Basic Go-To Easy Pizza Dough (here)
- ¼ cup Simple Tomato Sauce (here)
- ¼ cup shredded part-skim mozzarella cheese
- 1 tablespoon chopped fresh flat-leaf parsley
- Freshly ground black pepper

DIRECTIONS

1. Snap the woody ends off the asparagus, and with a vegetable peeler remove some of the tough skin on the lower end of the spears. Cut the spears on the bias into 2-inch-long segments. Toss with a little olive oil and salt and roast in a small cast iron skillet for 2 to 3 minutes.

2. Quarter the head of radicchio and cut out the stem and core from the wedges. Cut each wedge crosswise into ½-inch-thick ribbons. Transfer to a bowl and toss with a little olive oil, the red

wine vinegar, and 1 teaspoon of salt. Transfer to a cazuela and roast in the oven, turning and tossing, until wilted and somewhat browned, 5 to 7 minutes.
3. Drain and transfer the prepared artichokes to a cazuela, drizzle with olive oil and salt, add a splash of water, and roast in the window of the oven until tender, 5 to 7 minutes.
4. Following the directions for a fully prepped oven, make sure your fire is at the desired cooking temperature with a roiling flame and a brushed and cleaned oven floor. You are now ready to make a calzone.
5. Begin by dusting your work surface with a small amount of flour. Stretch the pizza dough by hand to a thin disc as described in "How to Shape a Pizza" (here). Dust the dough with a small amount of flour, turn over, and dust the other side. Using a rolling pin, gently roll the dough into a large, even, very thin circle. Continue to roll the dough, adding more flour as needed to prevent sticking. Transfer the dough to a lightly floured pizza peel.
6. Build the calzone on the half of the dough closest to you, as it will be folded over to create a half-moon shape. Spread the tomato sauce over the dough. Be sure to leave a 1-inch border to allow for a proper seal. Next, layer the shredded cheese, followed by the asparagus, artichokes, and finally ½ cup roasted radicchio. Sprinkle the chopped parsley over the ingredients and add a few grinds of black pepper.
7. In one quick motion, grasp the upper, undressed portion of dough and fold it over to meet the opposite edge, creating a half moon. Starting at one edge, seal the dough by pinching and rolling it over onto itself. Continue until the calzone is sealed. Tear a 1-inch hole in the top of the dough to release steam when baking.
8. Slide the calzone directly onto the oven floor and bake, rotating once or twice, until it is nicely puffed and browned, 7 to 10 minutes. Remove from the oven and brush the entire calzone with a small amount of olive oil to give it a glossy shine.

SPINACH, FETA, TAPENADE, AND OREGANO

MAKES ONE 8-INCH HALF-MOON CALZONE

Prep time: 20 minutes

Cook time: 7 to 10 minutes

Ingredients

- 1 portion Basic Go-To Easy Pizza Dough (here)
- ¼ cup Tapenade (here)
- ¼ cup part-skim mozzarella cheese, shredded
- 2 ounces feta cheese, drained and crumbled
- 1 cup spinach leaves, stems removed
- 1 red onion, thinly sliced on a mandoline, dressed with olive oil and salt
- 1 tablespoon pine nuts, lightly toasted

- 1 teaspoon oregano, oven-dried (see Prep Tip here) or fresh
- Freshly ground black pepper
- Extra-virgin olive oil

DIRECTIONS

1. Following the directions for a fully prepped oven, make sure your fire is at the desired cooking temperature with a roiling flame and a brushed and cleaned oven floor. You are now ready to make a calzone.
2. Begin by dusting your work surface with a small amount of flour. Stretch the pizza dough by hand to a thin disc as described in "How to Shape a Pizza" (here). Dust the dough with a small amount of flour, turn over, and dust the other side. Using a rolling pin, gently roll the dough into a large, even, very thin circle. Continue to roll the dough, adding more flour as needed to prevent sticking. Transfer the dough to a lightly floured pizza peel.
3. Build the calzone on the half of the dough closest to you, as it will be folded over to create a half-moon shape. Spread the tapenade over the dough. Be sure to leave a 1-inch border to allow for a proper seal. Next, layer the mozarella and feta cheeses, followed by the spinach, red onion, and pine nuts. Sprinkle the oregano over the filling and season with freshly ground pepper.
4. In one quick motion, grasp the upper, undressed portion of dough and fold it over to meet the opposite edge, creating a half moon. Starting at one edge, seal the dough by pinching and rolling it over onto itself. Continue until the calzone is sealed. Tear a 1-inch hole in the top of the dough to release steam when baking.
5. Slide the calzone directly onto the oven floor and bake, rotating once or twice, until it is nicely puffed and browned, 7 to 10 minutes. Remove from the oven and brush the entire calzone with a small amount of olive oil to give it a glossy shine.

STUFFED AND ROLLED PIZZA RING

MAKES ONE 10-INCH RING CALZONE

Prep time: 20 minutes

Cook time: 7 to 10 minutes

Ingredients

- 1 portion Basic Go-To Easy Pizza Dough (here)
- 2 tablespoons Essential Garlic Oil (here)
- ½ cup Simple Tomato Sauce (here)
- ¼ cup shredded part-skim mozzarella cheese
- ½ cup crumbled, cooked fennel sausage (see Prep Tip here)
- 2 tablespoons grated pecorino romano
- 1 teaspoon oregano, oven-dried (see Prep Tip here) or fresh
- Salt

- Freshly ground black pepper
- Extra-virgin olive oil

DIRECTIONS

1. Following the directions for a fully prepped oven, make sure your fire is at the desired cooking temperature with a roiling flame and a brushed and cleaned oven floor. You are now ready to make a calzone.
2. Begin by dusting your work surface with a small amount of flour. Stretch the pizza dough by hand to a thin disc as described in "How to Shape a Pizza" (here). Dust the dough with a small amount of flour, turn over, and dust the other side. Using a rolling pin, thinly roll the dough into a 10-inch round, adding more flour as needed to prevent sticking. Transfer the dough to a lightly floured pizza peel.
3. To build the ring, spread the garlic oil evenly over the dough, followed by the tomato sauce. Next, layer the shredded mozzarella, followed by the crumbled sausage, and then the pecorino romano. Sprinkle the oregano over the filling and season with salt and black pepper.
4. Starting at one edge, roll up the dough as if you're making a jelly roll and seal the edges by pinching them down. Turn the entire log over so the seam side is down. Gather both ends and connect them by lightly pinching together. Shape into a ring, taking care not to over-handle the dough or puncture it. Clean the peel of any **ingredients** that might prevent it from easily sliding in the oven.
5. Slide the ring directly onto the oven floor and bake, rotating once or twice and moving the ring through hot and cool zones to get even browning, until it is nicely puffed and browned, 7 to 10 minutes. Remove from the oven and brush the entire ring with a small amount of olive oil to give it a glossy shine. Allow to cool slightly before cutting into wedges.

WINE GRAPE FOCACCIA

MAKES ONE 12-BY-16-INCH FLATBREAD

Prep time: 2 hours

Cook time: 20 to 30 minutes

Ingredients

- 1 recipe Rosemary Focaccia ,reducing the fresh rosemary to ¼ cup
- 3 cups fresh wine grapes, such as Zinfandel or Pinot Noir or Concord, stemmed
- Flaked sea salt

DIRECTIONS

1. After you have topped the focaccia dough with the olive oil and rosemary, distribute the wine grapes evenly over the entire pan and gently press into the dough. The schiacciata is now ready for the oven.
2. To bake the schiacciata, allow a medium-hot fire to burn down so it is no longer flaming. A

nice mass of glowing embers and a fully heated oven is best. A slow steady bake is ideal here to prevent over-browning. If you have a laser thermometer, you are looking for a floor temperature of around 425°F. Insert the half sheet opposite the fire source and bake until the schiacciata is puffed and deep golden. Approximately 20 minutes of baking should set the dough; depending on your fire, it may take another 10 minutes.

3. Remove the pan from the oven and allow it to cool slightly. With a sharp knife cut around the dough and release it from the pan in one slab. The parchment paper should still be on the baked schiacciata, but if it isn't, don't fret.
4. Slide the dough back onto the warm oven floor for a final bake of the dough. This ensures a nice, evenly crispy crust. If you feel your schiacciata is sufficiently baked to your liking, omit this final step. Top with a generous sprinkling of flaky salt.
5. Transfer to a cooling rack. When cool, invert and peel off the parchment paper. I like to cut my schiacciata into large wedges or rectangular "fingers" that I can wrap in a napkin and pass to my guests as they enjoy a glass of wine.

SWEET HAND PIE OF PUMPKIN, WARM SPICES, AND MASCARPONE

MAKES TWO 6-INCH HAND PIES

Prep time: 45 minutes, plus overnight for chilling

Cook time: 6 to 8 minutes

Ingredients

- 1 recipe Sweet Dough for Hand Pies (here)
- ½ cup pumpkin purée
- ¼ teaspoon ground nutmeg
- ¼ teaspoon ground cinnamon
- Pinch ground cloves
- 1 teaspoon pure vanilla extract
- 2 tablespoons bourbon (optional)
- ½ cup mascarpone cheese
- ¼ cup granulated sugar, plus more for topping the pie
- Salt
- 1 egg yolk
- 1 tablespoon whole milk
- ½ cup (1 stick) unsalted butter, melted
- Powdered sugar (optional)

DIRECTIONS

1. Wrap the dough and shape into a thin, flat rectangle. This will make rolling the chilled dough

easier. Chill overnight in the refrigerator. The next day, roll the dough on a lightly floured surface and cut into two 5½-by-4¼-inch rectangles. Chill or freeze until ready to use.

2. In a medium bowl, combine the pumpkin purée with the nutmeg, cinnamon, cloves, vanilla, and bourbon, if using. In another bowl, combine the mascarpone and the granulated sugar and stir to dissolve.

3. Arrange a piece of dough with the shorter side closest to you. Spread half of the sweetened cheese on the bottom half of the dough, leaving a 1-inch margin from the edge of the dough. Top the mascarpone with half of the pumpkin mixture. Sprinkle on a pinch of salt.

4. Whisk together the egg yolk and milk. Brush the three exposed edges of the dough with the egg wash and fold the top half of the dough over the filling. Seal by pressing lightly with the back of a fork. Brush the entire pastry with melted butter and sprinkle over a little granulated sugar. With a sharp knife, make a slash or two on the top of the pie to release steam. Repeat with the other pie.

5. Refrigerate both pies for at least 15 minutes or up to 4 hours before baking.

6. Transfer the pies to a floured peel and bake in a moderate oven until the pastry is well colored and the filling is warmed through, 6 to 8 minutes. Cool slightly before enjoying. Dust with powdered sugar if desired.

SWEET HAND PIE OF ROASTED STONE FRUITS AND FRANGIPANE

MAKES TWO 6-INCH HAND PIES

Prep time: 45 minutes, plus overnight for chilling

Cook time: 6 to 8 minutes

Ingredients

- 1 recipe Sweet Dough for Hand Pies (here)
- 1 pound fresh stone fruits
- 1 vanilla bean, split, seeds scraped out
- ¼ cup granulated sugar, plus more for topping the pie
- 2 tablespoons frangipane
- 2 tablespoons sliced almonds, toasted
- 1 egg yolk
- 1 tablespoon whole milk
- ½ cup (1 stick) unsalted butter, melted
- Powdered sugar (optional)

DIRECTIONS

1. Wrap the dough and shape it into a thin, flat rectangle. This will make rolling the chilled dough easier. Chill overnight in the refrigerator. The next day, roll the dough on a lightly floured

surface and cut into two 5½-by-4¼-inch rectangles. Chill or freeze until ready to use.

2. Cut the fruit in half and remove the pits. Cut each half into 2 or 3 wedges, or more if the fruit is large. Transfer to a bowl and add the vanilla seeds and granulated sugar. Toss to combine. Transfer to a cazuela and roast in a hot oven until soft, bubbly, and slightly colored, 3 to 5 minutes. Do not overcook the fruit to the point where it entirely breaks down. Taste and adjust with more sugar if needed. Cool completely before using.

3. Arrange a piece of dough with the shorter side closest to you. Spread half of the frangipane on the bottom half of the dough, leaving a 1-inch margin from the edge of the dough. Top with ¼ cup roasted stone fruit and 1 tablespoon sliced almonds.

4. Whisk together the egg yolk and milk. Brush the three exposed edges of the dough with the egg wash and fold the top half of the dough over the filling. Seal by pressing lightly with the back of a fork. Brush the entire pastry with melted butter and sprinkle over a little granulated sugar. With a sharp knife, make a slash or two on the top of the pie to release steam. Repeat with the other pie.

5. Refrigerate both pies for at least 15 minutes or up to 4 hours before baking.

6. Transfer to a floured peel and bake in a moderate oven until the pastry is well colored and the filling is warmed through, 6 to 8 minutes. Cool slightly before enjoying. Dust with powdered sugar if desired.

SWEET HAND PIE OF ROASTED CHERRIES WITH GRAPPA AND AMARETTI

MAKES TWO 6-INCH HAND PIES

Prep time: 45 minutes, plus overnight for chilling

Cook time: 6 to 8 minutes

Ingredients

- 1 recipe Sweet Dough for Hand Pies (here)
- 1½ pounds fresh cherries
- 1½ tablespoons grappa (optional)
- 1 vanilla bean, split, seeds scraped out
- ¼ cup granulated sugar, plus more for topping the pie
- Salt
- 2 tablespoons frangipane (see A Closer Look here)
- 3 tablespoons amaretti cookie crumbs
- 1 egg yolk
- 1 tablespoon whole milk
- ½ cup (1 stick) unsalted butter, melted

- Powdered sugar (optional)

DIRECTIONS

1. Wrap the dough and shape it into a thin, flat rectangle. This will make rolling the chilled dough easier. Chill overnight in the refrigerator. The next day, roll the dough on a lightly floured surface and cut into two 5½-by-4¼-inch rectangles. Chill or freeze until ready to use.
2. Stem and pit the cherries and toss with the grappa, if using, the vanilla bean pod and seeds, and the granulated sugar. Add a pinch of salt. Transfer to a cazuela and roast the cherries until they soften and become slightly syrupy, about 5 minutes. Stir once or twice to avoid burning the fruit. Allow to cool before making the hand pies. Discard the vanilla bean pod. You should end up with about ½ cup cooked cherries.
3. Arrange a piece of dough with the shorter side closest to you. Spread half of the frangipane on the bottom half of the dough, leaving a 1-inch margin from the edge of the dough. Spread half of the cooked cherries and top with half of the amaretti crumbs.
4. Whisk together the egg yolk and milk. Brush the three exposed edges of the dough with the egg wash and fold the top half of the dough over the filling. Seal by pressing lightly with the back of a fork. Brush the entire pastry with melted butter and sprinkle over a little granulated sugar. With a sharp knife, make a slash or two on the top of the pie to release steam. Repeat with the second pie.
5. Refrigerate both pies for at least 15 minutes or up to 4 hours before baking.
6. Transfer to a floured peel and bake in a moderate oven until the pastry is well colored and the filling is warmed through, 6 to 8 minutes. Cool slightly before enjoying. Dust with powdered sugar if desired.

SWEET HAND PIE OF BLISTERED APRICOTS, RICOTTA, AND BITTERSWEET CHOCOLATE

MAKES TWO 6-INCH HAND PIES

Prep time: 45 minutes, plus overnight for chilling

Cook time: 6 to 8 minutes

Ingredients

- 1 recipe Sweet Dough for Hand Pies (here)
- 1 pound fresh apricots
- ¼ cup granulated sugar, plus more for topping the apricot halves and pies
- 1 vanilla bean, split, seeds scraped out
- ¼ cup plus 2 tablespoons fresh whole-milk ricotta cheese

- 3 tablespoons roughly chopped bittersweet chocolate
- 3 tablespoons toasted, chopped unsalted pistachios
- 1 egg yolk
- 1 tablespoon whole milk
- ½ cup (1 stick) unsalted butter, melted
- Powdered sugar (optional)

DIRECTIONS

1. Wrap the dough and shape it into a thin, flat rectangle. This will make rolling the chilled dough easier. Chill overnight in the refrigerator. The next day, roll the dough on a lightly floured surface and cut into two 5½-by-4¼-inch rectangles. Chill or freeze until ready to use.
2. Split the apricots in half and remove the pits. Arrange in a cazuela, cut-side up, and top with a sprinkle of granulated sugar, a splash of water, and the vanilla bean pod and seeds. Roast the fruit next to the coals in a very hot oven so the cooking goes quickly and color develops rapidly. I don't mind a little char on the fruit in this case. Discard the vanilla bean pod.
3. Combine the ricotta and the granulated sugar and stir to dissolve. Fold in the chocolate. Chill until ready to use.
4. Arrange a piece of dough with the shorter side closest to you. Spread half of the sweetened cheese on the bottom half of the dough, leaving a 1-inch margin from the edge of the dough. Top with 2 or 3 blistered apricot halves, cut-side down. Sprinkle over half of the chopped pistachios.
5. Whisk together the egg yolk and milk. Brush the three exposed edges of the dough with the egg wash and fold the top half of the dough over the filling. Seal by pressing lightly with the back of a fork. Brush the entire pastry with melted butter and sprinkle over a little granulated sugar. With a sharp knife, make a slash or two on the top of the pie to release steam. Repeat with the second pie.
6. Refrigerate both pies for at least 15 minutes or up to 4 hours before baking.
7. Transfer to a floured peel and bake in a moderate oven until the pastry is well colored and the filling is warmed through, 6 to 8 minutes. Cool slightly before enjoying. Dust with powdered sugar if desired.

WOOD-FIRED SHEEP'S MILK RICOTTA

MAKES 2 CUPS

Prep time: 10 minutes

Cook time: 10 to 15 minutes

Ingredients

- 1 pound fresh sheep's milk ricotta
- ½ cup extra-virgin olive oil
- 1 tablespoon salt

- Freshly ground black pepper
- Zest of 1 lemon, grated
- ½ cup Wild Fennel Sauce

DIRECTIONS

1. In a food processor, purée the ricotta, olive oil, salt, pepper, and lemon zest until smooth and whipped. Taste and adjust the seasoning as needed.
2. Spoon into a cazuela and smooth the top. Add the fennel sauce, if using, and spread evenly over the top of the smoothed cheese.
3. Bake in a moderate oven until lightly puffed and slightly browned on top, 10 to 15 minutes. Remove and let cool.
4. At this point the ricotta can be cut into wedges or spooned onto toasts or flat-bread and served as an appetizer.

WARM MONTRACHET WRAPPED IN GRAPE LEAVES WITH ROASTED WINE GRAPES AND FLATBREAD

SERVES 6 AS AN APPETIZER

Prep time: 10 minutes

Cook time: 4 to 5 minutes

Ingredients

- 2 (7-ounce) logs Montrachet or similar goat cheese
- 4 fresh grape leaves, washed and dried
- 1 large cluster wine grapes
- 1 tablespoon extra-virgin olive oil
- Salt
- North African Flatbread

DIRECTIONS

1. Wrap the grape leaves around the goat cheese and tuck in the loose ends. Transfer to a cazuela and set in the window of the oven. Roast just until softened and easily spreadable—it won't take long.
2. At the same time, toss the grape cluster with the olive oil and season with a bit of salt. Roast in a cast iron skillet for 4 to 5 minutes.
3. Enjoy the cheese and fruit paired with the crisp flatbread.

OVERNIGHT OVEN-DRIED TOMATOES SOTT'OLIO

MAKES 1 QUART

Prep time: 10 minutes

Cook time: overnight

Ingredients

- 2 pounds ripe tomatoes, such as Early Girl or Roma, halved, salted, and drained (see Prep Tip below)
- Salt
- Fresh herbs, such as rosemary, thyme, and oregano
- 3 cups extra-virgin olive oil

DIRECTIONS

1. When the oven has significantly cooled after a cooking session, rake the fire to break it up further. There should no longer be any flames and very few, if any, glowing coals. Allow the heat to dissipate for a few minutes.
2. Arrange as many half sheet pans as you like. Line them with cooling racks and place the tomatoes, cut-side up, snugly next to one another. Place the pans inside the cooling oven and set the door in place.
3. The next morning, retrieve the dehydrated, concentrated tomatoes and transfer to clean, dry mason jars. Pack the tomatoes fairly tightly, layering with herbs of your choice. Omit any tomatoes that have burned.
4. Cover the dried tomatoes with the olive oil and, using a chopstick or other utensil, try to release any trapped air among the layers by moving the tomatoes around so the oil fills the spaces where the air may have become trapped. Screw the lid on tightly and transfer to the refrigerator.
5. Over time the tomatoes will soften and the oil will take on the delicious flavor of the herbs and fruit. Enjoy both as part of an antipasto plate, on grilled bread, and of course on pizza.

GRATIN OF WILD MUSHROOM CRÈPES

MAKES 12 CRÈPES

Prep time: 10 minutes for the crèpes, 10 minutes for the filling, plus overnight for chilling

Cook time: 30 minutes for the crèpes, 5 minutes for the filling

Ingredients

FOR THE CRÈPES
- 2 cups whole milk
- ¼ cup (½ stick) unsalted butter
- Salt
- 1¾ cups all-purpose flour
- 4 extra-large eggs
- ¼ cup beer (optional)
- Canola oil

FOR THE FILLING
- 1½ pounds wild mushrooms such as porcini, morels, chanterelles, or black trumpets
- Salt
- 4 tablespoons (½ stick) unsalted butter, divided, plus more for the cazuela
- 4 tablespoons extra-virgin olive oil, divided
- 1 recipe Salsa Bianca (here)
- 2 garlic cloves, minced
- 2 tablespoons chopped fresh thyme
- ½ cup heavy cream
- ½ cup grated Parmesan cheese

DIRECTIONS

TO MAKE THE CRÈPES
1. In a small saucepan, warm the milk and butter together until the butter melts. Add a pinch of salt and set aside to cool slightly.
2. In the bowl of an electric stand mixer fitted with the whisk attachment, whisk the flour on low speed, then add the eggs all at once. Increase the speed to medium and whisk until combined and no lumps or flour remain visible. Lower the speed and slowly add the warm milk mixture, whisking constantly until combined.
3. Strain the batter through a fine-mesh strainer, pushing through any solids that remain. If the batter seems very thick, thin it with a few tablespoons of beer (if using) or milk. It should have the consistency of pancake batter. Refrigerate overnight.
4. Stir the crèpe batter well to combine anything that may have settled overnight. Grease a nonstick skillet or crèpe pan with a small amount of canola oil and heat over medium heat. Add 1 to 1½ ounces batter; simultaneously tilt and swirl the pan to get an even, thin pancake. Cook for 2 minutes, then flip the crèpe using a spatula or your fingers and cook for 30 seconds longer.
5. Slide the crèpe out of the pan, reheat the pan, and repeat until all of the batter has been used. Stack the cooked crèpes on top of one another and wrap in plastic wrap until ready to use, or freeze for up to 2 months.

TO MAKE THE FILLING
1. Clean and slice the mushrooms. Transfer to a dry kitchen towel to help absorb the excess

moisture.

2. Cook the mushrooms in four small batches so they sauté rather than steam. Season each batch with salt, and as the liquid they give off evaporates, add 1 tablespoon each of butter and oil per batch. Cook until they start to crisp and caramelize slightly, a few minutes longer. Remove to a plate and repeat with the other mushrooms, until all are cooked.
3. Transfer the mushrooms to a bowl and stir in enough salsa bianca to evenly coat them. Add the garlic and thyme.
4. Butter a large cazuela. Fill each crêpe with an equal amount of mushroom filling and fold over into a wedge. Transfer to the buttered pan. Lean each crêpe on the previous one to create a shingled pattern. Drizzle over the heavy cream and sprinkle the Parmesan cheese over all.
5. Bake in a moderately hot oven until the crêpes crisp, the cheese melts, and the filling is warmed through, about 5 minutes.

EGGPLANT ROASTED IN THE COALS

MAKES 1 CUP

Prep time: 10 minutes

Cook time: 30 to 40 minutes

Ingredients

- 2 medium globe eggplants
- 2 garlic cloves, mashed
- 2 tablespoons chopped fresh flat-leaf parsley
- 1 tablespoon chopped fresh mint
- 2 teaspoons ground coriander
- 1 teaspoon ground cumin
- Salt
- Freshly ground black pepper
- ½ cup extra-virgin olive oil
- Juice of 1 lemon

DIRECTIONS

1. Carefully fill a cast iron skillet with glowing embers. Using a metal peel works best to lift and deposit them into the pan. Place the eggplants directly in the coals in the skillet. Roast until very soft and blackened, 30 to 40 minutes, depending on their size, turning every so often.
2. Carefully remove the cooked eggplant to a heat-resistant tray and allow to cool until reasonable to handle.
3. Peel away the outer skin and scoop the flesh into a bowl. Or, if you prefer a smooth consistency, purée the flesh in a food processor.
4. Add the garlic, parsley, mint, coriander, cumin, salt, and pepper. Drizzle in the olive oil and balance the richness with the lemon juice and/or more salt.

ROASTED WINTER VEGETABLES IN DUCK FAT AND ROSEMARY

SERVES 6 AS A SIDE DISH

Prep time: 30 minutes

Cook time: 10 to 20 minutes

Ingredients

- 1 celery root, peeled and cut into 1-inch chunks
- 3 large parsnips, peeled and cut into 1-inch chunks
- 4 large carrots, peeled and cut into 1-inch chunks
- 12 small Tokyo turnips, or 1 large turnip, cut into 1-inch chunks
- 1 bulb fennel, cut into 1-inch chunks
- ¼ cup duck fat, melted
- 3 fresh rosemary sprigs, leaves stripped from the woody stems
- Salt

DIRECTIONS

1. Place the cut celery root, parsnips, carrots, turnips, and fennel in a bowl large enough to toss easily. Add the duck fat and rosemary, toss to thoroughly coat, season well with salt, and spread in a single layer on a half sheet pan.
2. Roast the vegetables in a moderate oven, rotating frequently and stirring to avoid burning, until they are tender, 10 to 20 minutes.

LONG-COOKED "POT O' BEANS" WITH OKRA, TOMATOES, AND PEPPERS

MAKES 4 CUPS OF BEANS

Prep time: 20 minutes

Cook time: 1 hour 10 minutes

Ingredients

- 8 tablespoons extra-virgin olive oil, divided
- 1 bay leaf

- 2 fresh thyme and/or savory sprigs
- 2 whole garlic cloves, peeled
- 3 cups fresh (or dried) shell beans such as cranberry, cannellini, or flageolet
- ½ yellow onion, cut in half
- 1 small fennel bulb, cut into 1-inch pieces
- 1 carrot, peeled and cut in half
- 1 cup okra, cut into 2-inch pieces
- 2 tomatoes, peeled, seeded, and diced
- 4 Jimmy Nardello peppers or 2 red bell peppers, seeded and diced
- Salt
- ¼ cup chopped fresh flat-leaf parsley or basil

DIRECTIONS

1. In a 4-quart pot, heat 2 tablespoons of olive oil on the stovetop, add the bay leaf and thyme or savory, then the garlic, and sauté gently for 30 seconds. Add the shell beans, onion, fennel, and carrot. Cover with water by 1 inch and bring to a boil. Lower the heat and slowly simmer until the vegetables are tender, 30 to 40 minutes.
2. Remove the cooked fennel and carrot and transfer the rest of the bean mixture to a cast iron pot with a tight-fitting lid. Add the okra, tomatoes, and peppers. Season with salt and add the remaining 6 tablespoons of olive oil, plus ½ cup to 1 cup water if the liquid level is low. Cover and place inside the doorway of the wood oven, next to the fire. Slowly cook until the tomatoes dissolve, the peppers are tender, and the okra has thickened the broth, 20 to 30 minutes.
3. Garnish with chopped fresh parsley or basil.

BAKED EGGS WITH TOMATOES AND DUKKA

SERVES 6

Prep time: 20 minutes

Cook time: 12 to 15 minutes

Ingredients

- 2 tablespoons extra-virgin olive oil
- 1 yellow onion, diced
- 4 ripe tomatoes, roughly chopped
- 2 garlic cloves, minced
- Salt
- 6 eggs
- 1 tablespoon chopped fresh flat-leaf parsley

- Freshly ground black pepper
- 1 tablespoon dukka (optional)

DIRECTIONS

1. Heat a cast iron skillet in the oven for 5 minutes, add the olive oil, and sweat the onion until soft and transparent. Add the chopped tomatoes and garlic and season with salt. Cook the tomatoes and onions until they concentrate and break down somewhat, 7 to 10 minutes, stirring occasionally.
2. Remove the pan from the oven and make 6 shallow depressions in the tomato-onion mixture. Crack the eggs individually into each depression and season with salt. Return to the oven and bake slowly until the whites are opaque and set and the yolks are runny, about 5 minutes. Garnish with chopped parsley, black pepper, and dukka, if using. Enjoy with toast.

SHRIMP COOKED IN THE WOOD OVEN WITH GARLIC AND OIL

SERVES 4 AS AN APPETIZER

Prep time: 20 minutes

Cook time: 3 to 5 minutes

Ingredients

- 1 pound fresh shrimp, peeled and deveined
- 4 garlic cloves, pounded to a paste in a mortar and pestle
- ½ cup extra-virgin olive oil
- Salt
- Freshly ground black pepper
- 1 teaspoon chili flakes
- ½ cup (1 stick) unsalted butter, cut in small pieces
- ¼ cup dry white wine
- Juice of 1 lemon
- ¼ cup chopped fresh flat-leaf parsley

DIRECTIONS

1. In a large bowl, toss the shrimp with the garlic and oil. Season with salt, a few grinds of black pepper, and the chili flakes. Arrange the shrimp in a cazuela, dot with butter, and pour over the white wine.
2. Transfer the prepared cazuela to a hot oven and roast until the shrimp are opaque and cooked through, 3 to 5 minutes. Remove from the oven, squeeze the lemon juice over the dish, and garnish with the chopped parsley.

CRACKED LOBSTERS ROASTED WITH PAPRIKA BUTTER

MAKES 2 LOBSTERS

Prep time: 30 minutes

Cook time: 5 to 7 minutes

Ingredients

- 2 whole live Maine lobsters
- 1 pound (4 sticks) unsalted butter, at room temperature
- 1 tablespoon sweet paprika
- 1 tablespoon smoked paprika
- 2 garlic cloves, smashed
- Zest and juice of 2 limes
- 2 teaspoons salt
- 1 tablespoon cognac

DIRECTIONS

1. Kill the lobsters by plunging a very sharp knife through the heads and set aside for 10 minutes in a bowl until they stop moving. Remove the claws and tail, reserving the body for another use.
2. In a pot of boiling water, cook the tails for 3 minutes and the claws for 5. Remove to a bowl filled with ice water. Drain and dry.
3. Split the tails in half, leaving the meat in the shell. Remove the knuckles from the claws and, with a small mallet, crack the shells all over.
4. Make the compound butter in the bowl of an electric stand mixer fitted with the paddle attachment. First soften the butter by beating it on medium speed for 3 minutes, then add both paprikas, the garlic, lime zest and juice, salt, and cognac, and beat until smooth. Taste and adjust with more of everything, if needed.
5. Spread the shellfish out in a single layer on a half sheet pan. Smear three-quarters of the soft compound butter over the meat and shells, working it into the cracks made by the mallet.
6. Roast the shellfish until it is sizzling and lightly colored, 5 to 7 minutes. Remove to a bowl and melt the reserved compound butter. Serve the lobster with the extra compound butter.

WHOLE ROASTED BRANZINO WITH TOMATOES, POTATOES, AND WHITE WINE

SERVES 4

Prep time: 25 minutes

Cook time: 20 to 30 minutes

Ingredients

- 2 large Yellow Finn potatoes, peeled and cut into ½-inch dice
- 12 fresh rosemary sprigs, divided
- 2 whole (1½-pound) branzino, cleaned
- Salt
- Freshly ground black pepper
- 1 lemon, thinly sliced
- ½ cup extra-virgin olive oil, divided
- ½ cup (1 stick) unsalted butter, cut in small pieces, divided
- 1 cup dry white wine, divided
- ½ cup cherry tomatoes
- ½ cup fish or chicken stock
- ¼ cup chopped fresh flat-leaf parsley

DIRECTIONS

1. Cook the potatoes in boiling salted water until tender, about 10 minutes. Drain well and reserve.
2. On a half sheet pan, scatter 8 of the rosemary sprigs. Season the inside of the fish cavities with salt and pepper, and stuff each with 2 rosemary sprigs and the lemon slices. Drizzle with ¼ cup of olive oil.
3. Season the outside of the fish with salt and pepper and place on top of the rosemary-lined sheet tray. Drizzle the entire platter with the remaining ¼ cup of olive oil. Dot with half of the unsalted butter, and pour over ½ cup of white wine.
4. Bake in a moderately hot oven, at least 500°F, rotating frequently and sliding closer to the mouth should the fish begin to darken too quickly. After 10 minutes, remove the tray and scatter the cherry tomatoes and cooked potatoes around and about the fish. Return to the oven and cook until the fish is somewhat translucent near the backbone, another 10 to 20 minutes.
5. When done, use a large spatula to remove the branzino to a waiting platter, scatter the vegetables around, and discard the rosemary branches from the pan.
6. Add the remaining ½ cup of wine, the remaining butter, and the stock to the pan, and use a

wooden spoon to scrape up any bits that may have become stuck. Return the pan to the oven to heat through and reduce slightly. Add the chopped parsley to the sauce.

7. For each fish, remove the top fillet, then the spine, and finally the bottom fillet. Dig the cheek flesh out of the head, just below the eye. Serve with the roasted vegetables and pan sauce poured over.

CANNELLONI WITH SPINACH, LEEKS, AND CHICKEN

SERVES 4

Prep time: 30 minutes for the pasta, 30 minutes for the cannelloni

Cook time: 25 minutes

Ingredients

FOR THE PASTA
- 1 cup 00 flour
- 1 extra-large egg plus 1 extra-large egg yolk
- 1 tablespoon extra-virgin olive oil

FOR THE CANNELLONI FILLING
- 3 tablespoons unsalted butter, divided
- 2 tablespoons water
- 1 cup thinly sliced leeks
- 1½ pounds ground chicken
- Salt
- 4 cups spinach leaves
- 2 cups Salsa Bianca (here)
- 1 cup shredded part-skim mozzarella, divided
- ½ cup heavy cream, divided
- 1 cup grated Parmesan cheese
- Freshly ground black pepper

DIRECTIONS

TO MAKE THE PASTA
1. Put the flour in the bowl of an electric stand mixer fitted with the paddle attachment. Add the egg, egg yolk, and olive oil and mix on low speed until the dough comes together. If it seems too dry, add a few drops of water.
2. Turn the dough out onto a lightly floured countertop and knead until it forms a slightly sticky ball. Wrap tightly in plastic wrap and let rest for 30 minutes.

3. Cut the dough ball in half and cover one half with plastic wrap. Using a pasta machine, gradually sheet the dough on the second to last setting on your machine, to retain an "al dente" bite after cooking. Repeat with the second half of the dough.

TO MAKE THE CANNELLONI

1. In a large sauté pan, melt 2 tablespoons of the butter with the water and sweat the leeks over medium heat until tender and transparent, 8 to 10 minutes. Add the ground chicken and cook thoroughly, about 5 minutes. Season with salt and transfer to a large bowl to cool.
2. Sauté the spinach in the remaining 1 tablespoon of butter until wilted, remove to a plate, and allow to cool. Squeeze out any excess moisture and roughly chop.
3. When the chicken is cool, add the Salsa Bianca and ½ cup of mozzarella. Mix well. Add the cooked spinach.
4. Bring a large pot of salted water to a boil. In the meantime, cut the sheeted pasta into eight 6-by-5-inch pieces. Have a bowl of ice water standing by and lay out a few clean towels on your kitchen counter. Cook the pasta sheets, a few at a time, for 2 to 3 minutes. Lift out with a large slotted spoon and drop into the ice water, then transfer to the towels and pat dry. Repeat the process until all the sheets have been cooked.
5. Gather a portion of the filling and roll it up in a pasta sheet, creating a tube. Wet the edges and seal. Transfer to a cazuela large enough to hold all eight cannelloni side by side, seam-side down. Repeat until all the pasta sheets and filling are used.
6. Brush some of the heavy cream over the rolled and filled pasta to moisten them and top with the Parmesan cheese and the remaining ½ cup of mozzarella. Season with salt and black pepper. Drizzle the remaining cream over the finished pasta rolls.
7. Bake in a moderately hot oven until the cheese melts and the pasta begins to brown and turns crispy, about 7 minutes.
8. Serve two cannelloni per person and spoon over the reduced cream.

VIETNAMESE-STYLE PORK SKEWERS IN LETTUCE CUPS

MAKES 10 TO 15 SKEWERS

Prep time: 30 minutes, plus overnight to marinate

Cook time: 5 to 7 minutes

Ingredients

- ¼ cup nuoc cham (Vietnamese fish sauce)
- ¼ cup minced fresh lemongrass, ground finely in a food processor
- ¼ cup chopped garlic
- ¼ cup peeled and grated galangal
- ¼ cup minced shallot

- 4 kaffir lime leaves
- 2 Thai bird or serrano chiles, sliced
- 2 tablespoons freshly ground black pepper
- 1 tablespoon sugar
- 1 tablespoon Thai five-spice powder
- 2 pounds boneless pork shoulder
- 15 lettuce leaves
- ½ cup torn fresh cilantro leaves
- ¼ cup finely chopped peanuts
- 2 limes, cut into wedges

DIRECTIONS

1. In a large bowl, combine the nuoc cham, lemongrass, garlic, galangal, shallot, kaffir lime leaves, chiles, black pepper, sugar, and five-spice powder.
2. Trim away any excess fat and gristle from the pork. Using a sharp knife, cut the pork into long, thin slices and add to the bowl. Mix the pork and the marinade well by hand. Cover with plastic wrap and refrigerate overnight.
3. The next day, remove the pork from the refrigerator at least 2 hours before you plan to cook it. Soak 15 wooden skewers in water for 1 hour.
4. Thread the pork slices onto the skewers. Transfer the skewers to a half sheet pan with the exposed wooden handles all facing the same direction. Do not overcrowd the skewers on the pan. When all the skewers are assembled, cover the exposed wooden handles with a sheet of aluminum foil to keep them from burning.
5. Transfer the skewers to the oven with the meat facing the fire. Cook until the pork browns and sizzles, remove from the oven, and use tongs to flip the skewers over. Return the protective foil to the handles and finish cooking on the other side. Cook for 5 to 7 minutes total.
6. Slide the skewers out of the pork and discard. Tuck each portion of pork into a lettuce cup, garnish with the cilantro and peanuts, and serve with a lime wedge.

RIB-EYE STEAK GRILLED "IN THE WINDOW" WITH SALSA VERDE

SERVES 2 AS A MAIN COURSE

Prep time: 1 hour

Cook time: about 15 minutes

Ingredients

- 2 tablespoons black peppercorns, crushed
- 1 (24-ounce) grass-fed, bone-in rib-eye or porterhouse steak, at room temperature
- 1 tablespoon salt

- 2 fresh rosemary sprigs, leaves stripped from the woody stems
- 2 tablespoons extra-virgin olive oil
- 1 recipe Salsa Verde

DIRECTIONS

1. Season the meat liberally with the salt and crushed peppercorns, pressing them into the flesh. Add the rosemary and rub the steak with the olive oil. Let it rest for 30 minutes.
2. Slide the grill into the mouth of the oven and rake a glowing, not flaming, bed of coals underneath the grill grate. Allow the grill to preheat for 10 minutes. Ideally, there will be a hotter section and a relatively cooler section of the grill; you will use both. Add the vine cuttings (if you have them) to the existing fire, away from the grill, to create smoke and flame while grilling.
3. Place the steak on the hottest part of the grill and leave for about 3 minutes to form a nice crust. Rotate the steak 90 degrees and continue to grill for 2 minutes longer. Flip the steak and repeat.
4. After 5 minutes, pull the steak to the cooler mouth area and grill a bit more slowly to your desired doneness. Medium-rare to rare is ideal, which will be about 15 minutes total. (By all means, grill the steak the way you like it.)
5. Remove the steak to a platter and allow to rest for 5 minutes before carving off the bone and slicing against the grain into ¾-inch-thick strips.
6. Garnish with the salsa verde and serve.

OVEN-ROASTED FRUITS

SERVES 4

Prep time: 10 minutes

Cook time: 5 to 7 minutes

FIGS ROASTED ON FIG LEAVES

Ingredients

- 2 fig leaves, washed and dried
- 8 fresh ripe figs, such as black Mission or Adriatic, stemmed and halved
- 2 tablespoons Chartreuse liqueur (optional)
- 2 tablespoons sugar

DIRECTIONS

1. In a cazuela, arrange the fig leaves and top with the cut fruit, stem ends pointing upward. Choose a vessel that fit the figs snugly, as this will prevent them from drying out. Add the liqueur, if using, and sprinkle on the sugar.
2. Roast in a moderate oven until softened and juicy, 5 to 7 minutes. Serve with cheese, over ice

cream, or alone.

CHERRIES ROASTED WITH KIRSCH AND CINNAMON

Ingredients

- 2 cups cherries, stemmed
- 2 tablespoons sugar
- 1 teaspoon ground cinnamon
- 2 tablespoons Kirsch (optional)

DIRECTIONS

1. In a bowl, combine the cherries, sugar, cinnamon, and Kirsch, if using.
2. Transfer to a cazuela and roast in a moderate oven, stirring once or twice to prevent burning, 5 to 7 minutes. Tell your guests to mind the pits!

APRICOTS ROASTED WITH DESSERT WINE AND VANILLA BEANS

Ingredients

- 8 apricots, halved and pitted
- ½ cup dessert wine, such as Sauternes or Beaumes de Venise
- ¼ cup sugar
- 2 vanilla beans, split

DIRECTIONS

1. In a cazuela, arrange the apricots, cut-side up. Pour over the dessert wine and sprinkle the sugar on top. Nestle the vanilla beans in and around the fruit.
2. Roast in a very hot oven for 5 to 7 minutes. Enjoy alone or in a sweet hand pie.

ESCAROLE, PERSIMMON, AND POMEGRANATE SALAD WITH TOASTED WALNUT VINAIGRETTE FALL

SERVES 6 TO 8

Prep time: 30 minutes

Cook time: 5 to 7 minutes

Ingredients

- 1 cup shelled walnuts
- Salt
- 6 teaspoons walnut oil, divided
- 1 shallot, minced
- 2 tablespoons Champagne vinegar
- 2 large heads escarole
- 2 cups arugula
- 3 heads Belgian endive, leaves separated and thinly sliced on the bias
- 1 tablespoon Dijon mustard
- ½ cup extra-virgin olive oil
- 2 Fuyu persimmons, peeled and very thinly sliced
- 1 cup pomegranate seeds (optional)
- Freshly ground black pepper
- Parmesan cheese (optional)

DIRECTIONS

1. Preheat the oven to 350°F.
2. Toast the walnuts on a baking sheet until light brown, 5 to 7 minutes. Wrap in a clean, dry dish towel and vigorously rub off the skins. Carefully remove the nuts from the towel and discard the skins. While the nuts are still warm, season with a pinch of salt and 2 teaspoons of walnut oil, and mix thoroughly. Set aside until ready to use.
3. In a small bowl combine the shallot with a generous pinch of salt and cover with the vinegar. Set aside for 10 minutes.
4. In a large bowl, toss together the escarole, arugula, and endive. Cover with a dish towel and refrigerate until ready to serve.
5. Add the mustard to the shallots and vinegar. Gradually whisk in the remaining 4 teaspoons of walnut oil, followed by the olive oil, in a slow, steady stream. Adjust the seasoning with more salt, vinegar, or olive oil as needed.
6. Remove the chilled chicories from the refrigerator and add the sliced persimmons and half of the seasoned walnuts. Sprinkle over the pomegranate seeds (if using), and gently and briefly mix the salad using both hands. Add half of the vinaigrette and toss again.
7. Taste a bit of all the components and adjust accordingly with more salt, oil, or vinegar. Garnish with the remaining nuts, give it a grind of black pepper, and shave wide ribbons of Parmesan cheese over the entire salad if you like. Pass the remaining vinaigrette for guests to enjoy.

SIMPLE ARUGULA AND HERB SALAD SPRING

SERVES 6 TO 8

Prep time: 10 minutes

Ingredients

- 1 pound arugula
- 2 tablespoons fresh lemon juice (from Meyer lemons, if available)
- Salt
- Freshly ground black pepper
- ⅓ cup extra-virgin olive oil
- 1 bunch fresh mint, leaves torn into rough pieces
- 15 fresh anise hyssop leaves, torn into rough pieces (optional)

DIRECTIONS

1. Put the arugula in a bowl large enough to facilitate tossing and dressing. Cover with a dish towel or damp paper towel and refrigerate until ready to use.
2. Put the lemon juice in a small bowl. Add a generous pinch of salt and several grinds of pepper. Whisk in the olive oil in a slow, continuous stream. Adjust the dressing with more salt or lemon juice. It should be bright and citrusy.
3. When ready to serve, sprinkle a generous pinch of salt over the arugula and add the mint and hyssop (if using). Toss by hand to distribute evenly. Drizzle half of the vinaigrette over the arugula and toss again until lightly coated. There should be no excess vinaigrette in the bottom of the bowl.
4. Taste and adjust with more salt or dressing as needed. Serve with the remaining vinaigrette on the side for guests to add to their liking.

FARM STAND VEGETABLE SALAD SUMMER

SERVES 6 TO 8

Prep time: 30 minutes

Ingredients

- 1 shallot, minced
- 2 tablespoons Champagne vinegar
- Salt
- ½ cup fresh green and/or purple basil leaves, plus 1 whole sprig
- 6 large, ripe tomatoes
- 1 large cucumber, peeled, seeded, and thinly sliced
- 2 large sweet peppers, cored and very thinly sliced
- 1 pint firm cherry tomatoes

- ⅓ cup extra-virgin olive oil
- 3 whole salt-packed anchovies, rinsed, soaked, and filleted (see Prep Tip here)
- 1 cup Aïoli (here), thinned with 1 tablespoon water
- Freshly ground black pepper

DIRECTIONS

1. Put the shallot in a small bowl, cover with the vinegar, and add a generous pinch of salt and the basil sprig. Let stand for 10 to 15 minutes.
2. Cut the large tomatoes crosswise into ¼-inch-thick slices and arrange on a wide, flat platter. Collect any tomato juice that may have escaped during slicing and spoon it over the slices. Season the tomato layer with salt.
3. In a large bowl, toss together the sliced cucumber and peppers, season with a pinch of salt, and scatter them over the tomato slices. Halve the cherry tomatoes, season with a pinch of salt, and let stand while you make the vinaigrette.
4. Remove and discard the macerated basil sprig from the shallots and vinegar. Whisk in the olive oil. Spoon the dressing over the entire vegetable platter. Scatter with the halved cherry tomatoes and their juice.
5. Slice the anchovy fillets lengthwise and distribute evenly over the salad.
6. Finally, tear the basil leaves into 1-inch pieces and garnish the platter. Drizzle the aïoli over all of the vegetables and herbs, or serve it on the side for guests to dress their own salads. Finish with a few grinds of black pepper.

LACINATO KALE SALAD WITH CREAMY GARLIC DRESSING AND RADISHES
WINTER

SERVES 6 TO 8

Prep time: 30 minutes

Cook time: about 5 minutes

Ingredients

- 3 bunches Lacinato kale, stems removed
- 1 egg yolk
- 1 teaspoon water
- 1 cup extra-virgin olive oil
- Juice of 1 lemon
- ¼ cup cream

- Salt
- 2 garlic cloves, mashed to a paste in a mortar and pestle
- 2 whole salt-packed anchovies, rinsed, soaked, filleted (see Prep Tip here), and mashed to a purée in a mortar and pestle
- 1 cup grated pecorino romano cheese, divided
- Freshly ground black pepper
- ½ cup sliced French breakfast radishes

DIRECTIONS

1. Set up a pot with a tight-fitting lid and a steamer basket large enough to hold the kale after it has been washed and stripped from its stems. Add just enough water to reach below the bottom of the basket. Don't overcrowd the steamer; rather, work in several small batches if necessary and steam the kale for about 2 minutes, until all the kale has been barely wilted. Remove the kale to a dry dish towel and allow to cool and drain. Transfer the kale to a bowl suitable for dressing the salad and refrigerate until ready to use.
2. In a clean bowl, whisk together the egg yolk and water. Slowly add the olive oil, whisking constantly to create a thick mayonnaise and adding a squeeze of lemon juice to thin the mixture from time to time. When all of the oil has been added, whisk in the cream, a generous pinch of salt, the mashed garlic, and the anchovy purée. Adjust the mixture with a few drops of water. It should taste bright and acidic. The dressing should have the consistency of pancake batter—thin it with a bit more cream or a few drops of lemon juice if necessary.
3. Set the dressing aside for 5 minutes to allow the flavors to mingle, then add half of the grated cheese and a generous amount of black pepper. Refrigerate until ready to use.
4. When ready to serve, toss the kale with a generous pinch of salt, add just enough garlic dressing to evenly coat the leaves, and toss again. Add half of the remaining cheese and toss again. Garnish with the remaining cheese, a few grindings of black pepper, and the sliced radishes.

Printed in Great Britain
by Amazon